JOB SHARING

An Annotated Bibliography

by
THYRA K. RUSSELL

The Scarecrow Press, Inc.
Metuchen, N.J., & London
1994

British Library Cataloguing-in-Publication data available

Library of Congress Cataloging-in-Publication Data

Russell, Thyra Kaye, 1945-
    Job sharing : an annotated bibliography / by Thyra K. Russell
    p.   cm.
    Includes index.
    ISBN 0-8108-2826-X (acid-free paper)
    1. Job sharing--Bibliography.   I. Title.
    Z7164.L1R78 1994
    [HD5110.15]
    016.33125'72--dc20   93-45475

This book is dedicated
to the true sharers in my life --
my parents, my sisters, and especially my
husband Herb and my daughter Alicia.

Contents

Introduction

This annotated bibliography on job sharing is simultaneously the lengthiest and most accurate overview of the subject, with more than 825 sources describing various applications of job sharing as it has been practiced in the United States, Great Britain, Canada, Australia, and Ireland. Every entry has been verified through a hands-on process that ascertained both the accuracy of the bibliographic citation and the nature of the various discussions. The compiler has endeavored to make all annotations sufficiently complete as to offer a prospective reader a thorough analysis of job sharing as it has been practiced from the mid-1960s (when it began to receive limited use) through December 1991 (when this bibliography ends). Those seeking instant information concerning the utility of job sharing for particular disciplines and professions are referred to the index.

Job sharing is best described as a form of part-time employment in which one full-time job is divided by two people who voluntarily work part-time and share the responsibilities and benefits of one full-time position. For example, two elementary school teachers may decide to share a teaching position by splitting the day--one teaching in the morning, the other in the afternoon. They are both committed to teaching but have voluntarily opted for a reduction in work hours while maintaining half their salary and a portion of their fringe benefits. The sharing is either horizontal (each partner is responsible for the total job requirements) or vertical (each partner is responsible for a defined half of the job). The British often refer to the latter as job splitting or "twinning."

Job sharing should not, however, be confused with two other forms of alternative work: flextime--which is an alternative work schedule that allows employees freedom in choosing their arrival and departure times; and work sharing--which reduces the number of hours an employee works along with a reduction in salary. This latter plan (usually temporary, but not voluntary) is a way of avoiding layoffs and sharing the work among those already employed.

Because job sharing and part-time employment are frequently confused, it is important to make several significant distinctions as to what job sharing is and is not: job sharing is voluntary but often demands a good deal of communication and cooperation between sharers; it may involve a variety of salary schedules, depending on time spent on the job and skills of the partners. In other words, job sharing is a way of restructuring a position that cannot be made into discrete part-time positions. Pay is based on a salary, however, not an hourly wage. Finally, job sharing usually has fringe benefits, while part-time employment does not.

Although no accurate information is available on how many people might benefit from job sharing, the reader will soon note that virtually every segment of the workforce has already made at least some use of job sharing, including spouses and single parents who wish to work while raising a family; those over fifty-five who are contemplating retirement; those who wish to pursue educational opportunities; recent graduates seeking entry into the workforce; and those who desire more flexibility in their work and leisure time. Job sharing has also been appropriate for some individuals who for health reasons cannot work full-time.

Businesses of all sizes and governmental agencies whose purview includes questions of manpower and the changing nature of the American workforce are also taking advantage of job sharing. It has been used by some institutions seeking to remedy affirmative action deficiencies.

Whether or not a given employer agrees to implement job sharing depends on a number of variables, including the key question of how benefits will be divided: some job sharers receive no benefits; most share benefits fifty-fifty; some sixty-forty; while others (a distinct minority) receive the same benefits of full-time workers.

Once a job-sharing program has been initiated, its success depends on how well the job sharers communicate with one another: it is absolutely imperative to talk, leave notes, a diary, log, or other record showing what has been done and what needs to be done.

The type of communication will probably depend on how an individual job is shared: some sharers each work half a day, some half a week, and some overlap; others divide a job on a 25-to-75 percent basis; and still others alternate by working a week, three months, and even six months. Three people can share a job as well as two. In certain high-stress professions (such as certain types of law), a forty-hour workweek may represent "job sharing"--down from the eighty hours per week practiced by others in a firm.

While it is probably impossible to determine when the first job-sharing plan was formulated, the earliest mention in this study (item No. 306) came when young Gaylord Nelson--later a U.S. senator from Wisconsin who would preside over Senate hearings on changing patterns of work (item No. 812)--decided he wanted to spend less time in a cannery (and more time on a beach) and proposed a job-sharing plan to his employer. He was routinely turned down, thereby illustrating two central precepts of job sharing: employers usually have to be "sold" on the idea; and those who propose job sharing should have both a dependable job-sharing partner in mind as well as solid plans for how the two will communicate.

In preparing this bibliography, exhaustive use was made of several sources. CD-ROM periodical databases checked regularly included the following: *Business Periodical Index, Library Literature, Dissertation Abstracts International, ERIC,* and *Education Index.* Online reference services used were these: INFOTRAC (which included the General Periodicals Index, the Expanded Academic Index, and the National Newspaper Index), CARL UnCover, and OCLC's FirstSearch Catalog. Paper indexes included the *Canadian Periodical Index,* the *State Education Journal Index,* and newspaper indexes for *The Christian Science Monitor, The Washington Post, The Wall Street Journal,* and *The Chicago Tribune.* In addition, several bibliographies on alternative staffing and various work time options were identified, and every entry on the topic of job sharing was investigated. Of course, as books and articles were read, more sources were revealed.

The bibliography is divided into four principal parts: General, Business, Education, and Government. The first part includes overviews of job sharing and items of general interest. The second part includes items pertaining to job sharing in industry or business organizations. Education-related items are included in the third part, and items relating to governments (city, state, national) are included in the fourth part. A brief bibliography of unpublished documents--reports or special occasion booklets--follows, along with an addendum of lately discovered materials. Finally, a subject and author index of all items begins on page 189.

The compiler relied on the help of numerous individuals and groups in preparing this bibliography. When contacted directly, several organizations responded to requests for copies of articles. These include the following:

Administrative Management Society (Trevose, PA)
American Association of School Personnel Administrators
    (Sacramento, CA)
American Way (Magazine of American Airlines)
Association of Wisconsin School Administrators (Madison, WI)
Austin (TX) Chamber of Commerce
Banking Insurance and Finance Union (London)
Bristol (England) United Press
California State Personnel Board (Sacramento, CA)
Camden Magazine (London Borough of Camden)
The Christian Science Monitor
Christian Woman (Worthing, W. Sussex, England)
Colorado State University Libraries
Department of Recreation and Culture, City of Ottawa (Ontario)
Employment Department (Birmingham, England)
Equal Opportunities Commission (Manchester, England)
Evening Echo (Basildon, Essex, England)
Girl About Town Magazine (London)
Greater London Record Office, Head Archivist
Harvard University, Graduate School of Education (Cambridge, MA)
IPC Magazines, Ltd. (London)
Institute of Manpower Studies (Brighton, England)
Institute of Personnel Management (London)
International City Management Association (Washington, DC)
Jefferson County Teachers Association (Louisville, KY)
Library Association (London)
London Residuary Body
Michigan Department of Civil Service, Office of Policy & Public
    Affairs (Lansing)
Modern Records Centre, University of Warwick Library (Coventry,
    England)
National and Local Government Officers Association (London)
National Association of Probation Officers (London)
National Magazine Company, Ltd. (London)
National Union of Teachers (London)

New Ways to Work (London)
New Ways to Work (San Francisco)
The New York Times
NextStep Publications (Seattle, WA)
Office of Personnel Management, State of Utah
Office of Personnel Services, Department of Education, State of
    Hawaii
Office of the Legislative Auditor, State of Hawaii
Ontario Ministry of Labour Library (Toronto)
Oregon Department of Education (Salem)
Oxford (England) *Mail*
Oxford (England) *Times*
Permanent Commission on the Status of Women (Hartford, CT)
Portland (OR) Chamber of Commerce
Recreation & Community Services (City of Campbell, CA)
Royal Institute of Public Administration (London)
Sacramento (CA) *Bee*
Saskatchewan (Canada) Teachers' Federation
Sheffield (England) City Council
Shell UK Administrative Services (London)
Smithsonian Institution Women's Council (Washington, DC)
Social Planning Council of Metropolitan Toronto
Swarthmore (PA) College
Wichita (KS) Public Schools
Woman and Home (London)
Women's Bureau, U.S. Department of Labor

In addition, this bibliography could not have been completed without the special assistance of many colleagues within Library Affairs at Southern Illinois University at Carbondale, especially the Dean, Carolyn A. Snyder, the Assistant to the Dean, Mark Watson, the Director of Technical and Automation Services, Jay Starratt, and Humanities Librarian, Loretta Koch. The compiler relied heavily on personnel in Access Services, especially Thomas L. Kilpatrick, Tammy Winter, and David Brossart, who processed the numerous interlibrary loan requests. Former Order Librarian Betty Hutton also offered support and assistance. The compiler also received continual encouragement and superior support from her own staff: Jeffery Agne, Rose Clam, Donna Johnson, Nancy Mace, Avis Myers, Diane Roseman, and student assistants Karin McClure and Kari Sargeant in addition to student word processor Maria Castro.

General

1. *AMS Flexible Work Survey.* Trevose, PA: Administrative Management Society, 1986, 1987, 1988, & 1989.

   These annual surveys (suspended in 1990) report on a sampling of members of the Administrative Management Society by giving statistics on the respondents' use of flextime, part-time employment, compressed workweeks, and job sharing. The figures on job sharing are given by type of business (insurance, education, banking, utilities, manufacturing, and retail), by company size (1-10,000 employees), by region of the United States (Midwest, Great Lakes, Northeast, South, West) and Canada, and by type of benefits (vacation/sick pay, pensions, and medical insurance) job sharers receive.

2. *Adjusting Work Time: Three New Models.* San Francisco: New Ways to Work, 1978. 32p.

   Distinctions between work sharing, job sharing, and leave time are presented in this booklet along with examples of each. Bibliography.

3. *Alternative Work Schedules.* Boston: Allyn and Bacon, 1989. 223p.

   The differences between vertical and horizontal job sharing are described in the chapter entitled "Permanent Part-Time Employment."

4. Amir, Dale. *Job Sharing: A New Way to Work.* Edinburgh: Scottish Council of Social Service [1983]. 18p.

   Included are advantages and disadvantages of job sharing for both employees and employers. Also included is a section on initiating a job-sharing position, union involvement, and the government's response. Bibliography.

1

5.   Anderson, Judith. "Finding Jobs Two Can Share." *San Francisco Chronicle*, 18 November 1976, 31.

      People looking for part-time positions are encouraged by personnel from California's New Ways to Work firm that specializes in alternative work opportunities. The city of Palo Alto allows job sharing, as do many schools in the area.

6.   *Annotated Bibliography on Working Time*. Geneva: International Labour Office, 1986. 100p.

      Twenty-nine entries on the subject of job sharing are included in this annotated bibliography, which includes monographs, journal articles, reports, and conference proceedings.

7.   Arkin, William, and Lynne R. Dobrofsky. "Job Sharing." In *Working Couples*, edited by Rhona Rapoport and Robert N. Rapoport. London: Routledge and Kegan Paul, 1978, pp. 122-137.

      This chapter describes what job sharing means to couples who share marriage and work and how their employers view the arrangement. The authors surveyed twenty-one job-sharing couples, most of whom were teachers at the college or university level. Advantages are described in addition to situations that cause stress. Bibliography.

8.   _____. "Job-Sharing Couples." In *Working Women and Families*, edited by Karen Wolk Feinstein. Beverly Hills, CA: Sage Publications, 1979, pp. 159-175.

      This chapter is a result of research Arkin and Dobrofsky conducted on job-sharing couples in professional occupations: teachers, social workers, journalists, ministers, and administrators. Most of the job-sharing positions were the result of the unavailability of two jobs or the unwillingness of either the man or woman to compete for the same job or to commute to another city. Also included are the attitudes of employers toward job-sharing couples and the feelings of both the men and the women in these positions. Bibliography.

9.   Armstrong, Ann, and Bev Farrell. "Job Sharing: Benefiting the Employer and Staff Involved, but Most Importantly--the Volun-

teers and Agencies Served." *Voluntary Action Leadership* (Fall 1986): 24-26.

After extensively researching job sharing, colleagues working for the city of Bloomington, Indiana, propose job sharing for the directorship of the Volunteer Action Center. Acceptance by the mayor allowed them to put their plan into effect. They believe they operate more efficiently and effectively than one person working alone. A follow-up article on volunteer administrators sharing a job is described in item No. 82.

10.   Armstrong, Jill. "Share and Share Alike." *Yorkshire* (Leeds, England) *Post*, 27 April 1981, 8.

Several job-sharing couples report on the flexibility of their work arrangements. The London-based Job Sharing Project provides help and advice for people who want to share jobs.

11.   *Articles and Reports on Job Sharing.* Palo Alto, CA: New Ways to Work [1981. 25p.].

This is a collection of newspaper and journal articles that have been reprinted and published under one title. Most are individually annotated in this bibliography.

12.   Askari, Emilia. "Drake Project Helps Promote Job Sharing." *Des Moines* (IA) *Sunday Register*, 1 August 1982, F10.

Drake University's Project Job Share is an Iowa-state-funded project designed to show managers and those interested in part-time work how job sharing can benefit them both. Examples of workers who have taken advantage of the program are given.

13.   Bagchi, Pat. "Job Sharing." *Peninsula Magazine* 1 (April 1976): 12-15.

Job sharing is shown to work at several places in California: Stanford University, Palo Alto Unified School District, and in city government positions in Palo Alto.

14.   Baker, Nancy C. "Divide and Conquer: How Job Sharing Works." *Working Mother* 5 (January 1982): 14+16+18+92-93.

Job sharing is described as a work option enjoyed by many women who wish to work part-time and also be at home raising their children. Women in various employment positions describe their "ideal" situations and why it is important to them.

15. Barkas, Janet. "A New Trend: Job Sharing." *McCall's* 102 (November 1974): 56.

Women employees are pairing up with another person and persuading employers to hire them to fill one position. Tips are given on finding a partner, interviewing, and dividing benefits.

16. Barr, Pat. "Two for the Price of One: A New Way to Work." *Good Housekeeping* (British ed.) (June 1979): 76-77+218+220.

Barr examines how and where job sharing is working in the London area. She describes several jobs that are shared by women and includes one position filled by two men--a field officer's job with the International Voluntary Service in Yorkshire, England.

17. Barrington, Eleanor. "The New Wave: The Part-Time Work Compromise." *Today's Parent* 6 (April/May 1989): 30-32+34.

Canadian employees are discovering that part-time work has more advantages than disadvantages. Job sharing is one way for part-time professionals to keep up with their careers.

18. Benderly, Beryl Lieff. "How to Turn the Full-Time Job You Have into the Part-Time Job You Want." *Redbook* 156 (November 1980): 29+102+104-105.

Part-time work has advantages for some that are greater than full-time employment. Two career counselors describe the importance of a well-thought-out job-sharing proposal.

19. Bennett, Maureen V. "Job Sharing: State-of-the-Art and Feasibility as an Alternative Work Pattern." MBA thesis, Pace University, 1982. 136p.

Bennett's research is designed to address several matters, including why job sharing was instituted, where successful and unsuccessful sharing arrangements are found, problems, additional costs or costs savings, and plans for expansion. The primary goal of her study was "to dismiss the ambiguity present in the perceived problems associated with job sharing." Bennett conducted fourteen personal interviews with employees in both public and private sectors. She details the options at the state government level for fourteen states and seven county local governments. In addition to telling of job sharing in government, Bennett describes initiatives in the fields of medicine, education, and library science. The final chapter details the job-sharing experience itself--problems, salary, promotion, performance appraisal, fringe benefits, and reversibility as well as the qualitative benefits the employer enjoys, such as better morale, more creativity, more qualified applicants, job continuity, improved job satisfaction, and retention of valued employees. Bibliography.

20.   Bergsman, Steve. "Part-Time Professionals Make the Choice." *Personnel Administrator* 34 (September 1989): 49-52+105.

With a change in work and lifestyles, the part-time employee has become more prevalent. Women sharing a position at Chase Manhattan Bank in Lexington, Massachusetts, have very little overlap. Their job is split into separate functions and their duties are totally different.

21.   Berkman, Sue. "Half a Job Can Be Better Than One." *Savvy* 2 (March 1981): 14+18.

Shared jobs may result from restructuring an existing position or from people applying individually or jointly for one position. An example of a joint application letter is included.

22.   Blai, Boris. *"Creative" Work Schedules.* Bethesda, MD: ERIC Document Reproduction Service, 1988. 13p. ED 294 011.

This document describes how the creation of job-sharing positions is often the result of modifying or restructuring existing positions. Included is a section on analyzing cost-effectiveness. Bibliography.

23.   Blyton, Paul. "Reorganizing Working Time." *International Social Science Journal* 34 (1982): 149-156.

Perceptions of job sharing and part-time employment are discussed.

24.   *A Booklet of General Information about Job Sharing.* [Palo Alto, CA]: New Ways to Work, 1977. 15p.

This booklet describes in detail how hours can be arranged, advantages for employers, questions employers ask, and how benefits can be divided.

25. Boratynski, Marsha Leah. "Sex Role Differentiation and Equality in a Job-Sharing Family: A Participant Observation." Ph.D. diss., Michigan State University, 1980. 199p.

Boratynski's dissertation is a study of a job-sharing family in which the spouses divide the work load of a church pastor position. In addition to observing the family for one hundred hours, the researcher conducted extensive interviews with the sharers. Data analysis included the life histories of the family, a description of the family environment, the organization of work and family tasks, and the direction of role changes in family and work situations. Bibliography.

26. "Bosses' Doubts on Job Sharing." *Coventry* (England) *Evening Telegraph*, 13 February 1985, 15.

This article reports that job sharing is not economical for employees (who find it difficult to live on half a salary) or employers (who find that it increases their operating expenses).

27. Boyle, Adrienne. "Job Sharing and Work Sharing." *Local Government Chronicle* (London), 24 October 1980, 1123.

Boyle is writing a letter to the editor to clarify the differences in work sharing, job sharing, and "cutbacks."

28. Briscoe, Joanna. "Job Sharing." *Girl about Town Magazine* (25 January 1988): 52-53.

Briscoe features four women who are job sharers. Each describes her job (teaching or researching) and how it was set up. All report job sharing works well for them and has been supported by their employers and families.

29. Brosnan, Dolores. "Alternative Work Patterns in the Public Sector: Job Sharing as One Option." *International Journal of Public Sector Management* 2 (1989): 51-62.

The author reports that job sharing is a way in which full-time career employees can be hired on a part-time basis. She describes studies done in New York and Michigan that support the theory that alternative work schedules are wanted and needed not only by working mothers but by others interested in free time during the workday. Brosnan also describes the reported benefits of job sharing and details a job-sharing arrangement in an upstate New York YWCA where the position of executive director is shared. Bibliography.

30. Burrow, Margaret, and Maggie Reid. "Job Sharing: The Answer for Not-So-Stay-at-Home Mums." *Mother* (October 1980): 30-31.
    Several job-sharing teams describe how they got their positions and why they enjoy them. The London-based Job Sharing Project was established in order to research the concept of job sharing and to provide help to prospective job-sharing employees.

31. "Bye-Bye, 9 to 5." *Changing Times* 40 (February 1986): 88.
    Employees and employers both anticipate a change in the traditional working hours and think more people will volunteer to work part-time.

32. "Call on MAJ to Share Work." *Ashton-under-Lyne* (England) *Reporter*, 24 January 1986, 11.
    Manchester Area Job Sharers (MAJ) is a group of English volunteers intent upon establishing a resource center for potential job sharers.

33. Carter, Don. "Jobs Split When Living Expands: 'Pioneers' Seek End to 40-Hour Tyranny." *Seattle Post-Intelligencer*, 15 January 1978, F2.
    A nonprofit agency called Focus on Part-Time Careers is established in Seattle to explain the concept of job sharing and to help women and men who are interested in part-time employment.

34. Casner-Lotto, Jill. "Demand for Professional Part-Time Work Growing Faster in U.S. Than Openings; Private, Public Sectors Experimenting." *World of Work Report* 4 (October 1979): 74+78.

Permanent part-time work has become attractive to many and opportunities have increased. It has been demonstrated that job sharing can work well in professional positions.

35. Chambré, Susan M. "Job Sharing for Volunteers." *Voluntary Action Leadership* (Summer 1989): 24-25.

The author points out that job sharing can work with volunteer (unpaid) workers as well as it does for salaried employees. The teaming of an experienced volunteer with a novice is one of the ideas described in this article.

36. "Changing Work Patterns." *Management Review* 69 (March 1980): 4-5.

Job sharing is a departure from the traditional work pattern. Some sharers believe their productivity goes up because they have fewer hours in which to complete an assignment and they are forced to set goals.

37. Chapin, Vincent J. *Work Life and Personal Needs: The Job-Sharing Option.* Ottawa: Labour Canada, 1989. 31p.

Chapin prepared this monograph for the Canadian Women's Bureau because it had received many requests for information on job sharing. The book deals with prospects and problems from both the employers' and employees' perspectives. It tells how to arrange sharing a job and details several issues and concerns such as compensation, job content, exaggerated expectations of performance, duplication of effort, prospects for promotion, and performance reviews. Bibliography.

38. Chapman, Rhiannon. "Job Sharing: Fad or Fixture?" *Personnel Management* 15 (May 1983): 3.

The head of personnel at the London Stock Exchange defines job sharing, job splitting, and work sharing and explains the differences between job sharing at the Stock Exchange and the British government's job-splitting scheme.

39. Christensen, Kathleen. *Flexible Staffing and Scheduling in U.S. Corporations.* New York: Conference Board, 1989. 22p.

This survey describes various flexible staffing and scheduling arrangements reported by 521 companies (out of a possible 2,775) that were questioned about their use of several different work arrangements, including job sharing. Answers indicated that sharers are typically former full-time employees who change to a job-sharing status (which is often initiated by the employees). Benefit packages are usually the same as those received by regular part-timers. Whether job sharing is successful or not varies widely among firms.

40. _____. "Here We Go into the 'High-Flex' Era." *Across the Board* 27 (July-August 1990): 22-23.

Christensen reported in a survey she completed for the Conference Board that the most common alternative work arrangement was part-time employment but that one-fifth of the firms she surveyed offered job sharing.

41. Christopher, Jude, and Nadine Perry. "The Thoughts of Two Sharers." *Australian Society* (1 October 1983): 12.

These two authors have shared three different jobs and have found the experience satisfying--both from professional and personal viewpoints. They attribute their success to "complete trust, communication, mutual generosity, and non-competitiveness between workers as well as seeing themselves as equal parts of one job."

42. Clutterbuck, David. "Why a Job Shared Is Not a Job Halved." *International Management* 34 (October 1979): 45-47.

Board members of a community organization are surprised to receive a joint application from two women proposing to share the job of executive director. Acceptance is granted. Included in this article are several advantages that job sharers can emphasize during employment interviews.

43. "Coast Group Finds a Rise in Workers Sharing Jobs." *New York Times*, 26 September 1979, A15.

According to personnel at New Ways to Work located in San Francisco, job sharing developed because many career-oriented professional employees wanted part-time work.

44. Coberly, Sally. "Alternative Work Arrangements." In *Significant Segment Handbook 1: Employment and Training of the Mature*

Worker: A Resource Manual, edited by Dorothy Bauer, Victor S. Barocas, and Patricia Ferber-Cahill. Washington, DC: National Council on the Aging, 1982, pp. 85-104.

Alternative work schedules including job sharing offer the kind of flexibility wanted by many employees. Likewise, employers view alternatives to the traditional workweek as a way of solving management problems. Bibliography.

45. _____. "Keeping Older Workers on the Job." *Aging* (1985): 23-25+36.

Retaining older workers in the labor force has become important to employers as well as prospective retirees. Job sharing allows for retaining or rehiring individuals who have either retired or wish to phase into retirement.

46. Cohn, Bob. "A Glimpse of the 'Flex' Future." *Newsweek* 112 (1 August 1988): 38-39.

Untraditional work schedules allow both men and women to balance the demands of work and home. Steelcase, Inc., an office furniture company in Grand Rapids, Michigan, offers a variety of flexible schedules, including job sharing.

47. Coles, Margaret. "Pros and Cons of Job-Sharing Schemes." *Daily Telegraph* (London), 5 April 1986, 8.

Coles details job-sharing advantages and disadvantages and explains why the British government's job-splitting scheme has been criticized. Workers in clerical and administrative positions, including executives, doctors, librarians, and teachers, are participating in, and supportive of, job sharing.

48. Collins, Glenn. "Lawyers Share Jobs for More Family Time." *New York Times*, 9 July 1984, B6.

Lawyers in the New York State Attorney General's office prove that job sharing works. Even though some sharers may feel they are not moving up the career ladder as quickly as they wish, there is not a formal policy prohibiting job sharers from advancing.

49. Costanzo, Charlene Gorda. "Job Sharing." *McCall's* 109 (March 1982): 40.

Ways of approaching an employer about job sharing are
described in this article.

50. Cotterell, Alison. "Forward to the 17-Hour Week." *Guardian*
     (London), 23 April 1988, 33.
     Full-timers can reduce their working schedules without
     giving up a professional career by engaging in job sharing.
     Freelancers often find job sharing ideal because they are
     guaranteed a salary in addition to having free time needed to
     pursue other activities.

51. "Couple Start Job Sharing with a Difference." *Banstead*
     (England) *Advertiser*, 24 January 1985, 13.
     A married couple shares their government statistician
     position while also dividing child-care responsibilities.

52. Cowe, Roger. "Work Sharers Are Finding Friends on All Sides."
     Guardian (London), 25 September 1986, 24.
     Traditionally, job sharers have been women who want some
     free time to spend with their families. More recently, men have
     shown an interest in job sharing and it is affecting businesses in
     both the public and private sectors.

53. "Crusade to Ease Dole Money." *Oxford* (England) *Times*, 28
     June 1985, 1.
     In an effort to help unemployed workers obtain jobs, an
     Oxfordshire resident establishes her own no-charge job-sharing
     register.

54. Daly, Margaret. "A Flexible Work Plan for Married Women."
     Better Homes and Gardens 52 (January 1974): 6+9.
     Partnership employment began in the United States with
     experiments conducted by Catalyst, a nonprofit educational
     service for women who wanted an alternative to traditional work
     options. Catalyst, founded by Felice Schwartz, began work in
     the mid-1960s with partnership teachers in Framingham,
     Massachusetts, and social workers employed by the
     Massachusetts Department of Social Welfare.

55.   Deutschman, Alan. "Pioneers of the New Balance." *Fortune* 123
       (20 May 1991): 60-62+64+68.
       Deutschman reports that many career-minded employees are
       taking advantage of alternative work arrangements--part-time
       work, job sharing, leaves of absence, and working at home. In
       many cases, this has not prevented the employees' careers from
       prospering. Included here are reports from several professionals
       indicating that flexible schedules have enhanced their careers
       and helped them to balance work responsibilities with personal
       needs.

56.   Diggs, J. Frank. "Job Sharing: For Many, a Perfect Answer."
       U.S. News & World Report 93 (23 August 1982): 66-68.
       This article includes a wide variety of examples of why the
       number of part-timers has steadily increased and where job
       sharing is taking place.

57.   Dungate, Michaela. "Will Two into One Go?" *Initiatives*
       (August 1982): 4-6.
       Dungate reports on the British government's plan to
       alleviate unemployment via job splitting by explaining its effect
       on employees and employers, the costs and benefits, and the
       union involvement. Included is a report on a job-sharing
       experiment at GEC Telecommunications.

58.   Duttweiler, Robert W. *Job Sharing: An Alternative to
       Traditional Employment Patterns.* Bethesda, MD: ERIC
       Document Reproduction Service, 1982. 20p. ED 218 729.
       The distinctions between job pairing, job splitting, and job
       sharing are defined. Advantages and disadvantages to all those
       involved in job sharing are included along with predictions for
       the future. Bibliography.

59.   Dworaczek, Marian. *Alternative Work Schedules: A
       Bibliography, 1980-1986.* Monticello, IL: Vance Bibliographies,
       1987. 68p.
       This bibliography (not annotated) includes a section entitled
       job sharing and work sharing that lists over 200 items. The job-
       sharing entries are included individually in the present work.

60. "England: Job Sharing Proposed to Alleviate Shortages of Teachers, Nurses." *Work Times* 5 (Summer 1987): 3.

Recruiting difficulties have motivated some London employers to consider job-sharing options. A 10 percent increase in wages was suggested as a way of covering "overlap time."

61. English, Carey W. "Job Sharing Gains Ground Across U.S." *U.S. News & World Report* 99 (14 October 1985): 76.

While municipal and federal government offices, school districts, and nonprofit organizations are encouraging job sharing, private industry has not fully accepted it. Job sharing can mean higher costs for employers (depending upon unemployment compensation and benefit policies). Predictions for the future, however, include a rise in job-sharing practices.

62. Epstein, Joyce. "Issues in Job Sharing." In *New Forms of Work and Activity*, edited by Ralf Dahrendorf, Eberhard Köhler, and Françoise Piotet. Dublin: European Foundation for the Improvement of Living and Working Conditions, 1986, pp. 39-88.

Commissioned by the European Foundation for the Improvement of Living and Working Conditions, the author presents a comprehensive analysis of what job sharing is, why it is taking place, who is doing the sharing, the development of job sharing in Europe, and the impact of and potential demand for job sharing. Also included are European management and union attitudes toward job sharing. Bibliography.

63. Evans, Alastair. "Measures to Make the Jobs Go Round." *Personnel Management* 11 (January 1979): 32-35.

Job sharing is included as one option to alleviate the unemployment problem in the United Kingdom. The author views job sharing as suitable for older workers approaching retirement but also sees it attracting unexpected employees into the labor force, thus creating a negative effect on the reduction of unemployment.

64. "Expert Sees Growing Need for Employers to Back Job Sharing." *Savings & Loan News* 103 (January 1982): 84-85.

Reasons employers are becoming interested in job sharing are recounted by Barney Olmsted, co-director of New Ways to Work based in San Francisco, California.

65.   Fader, Shirley Sloan. "A Guide to Part-time Work." *Ladies' Home Journal* 101 (October 1984): 66+70-72.

Job sharing is one of the ways to meet the demands for part-time employment, but sharers must be willing to work together and cooperate--and remember that the nature of job sharing can make promotions and salary increases harder to obtain.

66.   Fiumara, Georganne. "Combining Kids and Career." *Family Circle* 102 (27 June 1989): 26+28-30+32.

Investment bankers with young sons presented a written plan to their department head requesting the opportunity to job share. Management approved the request. In addition to receiving full benefits, each woman was paid 60 percent of her previous full-time salary. This article also includes pointers on how to negotiate a flexible work option.

67.   Fletcher, Charlie, and Jan Fletcher. "Do Job Sharing and Flexible Work-Time Provide Balance for Young Families?" *New Families: A Journal of Transitions* 1 (Spring 1987): 6-9.

Flexible scheduling such as job sharing allows both mothers and fathers to balance family and career demands. This article includes information on the State of Wisconsin's Project JOIN (Job Options and Innovations), which established 118 shared positions in the late 1970s.

68.   *Flexible Patterns of Work*, edited by Chris Curson. London: Institute of Personnel Management, 1986. 340p.

This book covers flexible work arrangements of all kinds--flextime, compressed workweeks, shift working, sabbaticals, extended leaves, and alternatives to full-time work such as temporary, part-time, working at home, and job sharing. The section on job sharing includes policy guidelines for GEC Telecommunications in Coventry, the British Broadcasting Corporation, Fox's Biscuits in West Yorkshire, and the Irish Civil Service. Bibliography.

69.   *Flexible Scheduling for Managers and Professionals: New Work Arrangements for the 1990s.* Washington, DC: Bureau of National Affairs, 1990. 32p.

Information presented in this booklet is based on a report issued by Catalyst, an organization founded in 1962 to work toward change for women in business. Job sharing is one example of staffing flexibility that meets the needs of many company managers and professional employees.

70.   *Flexible Work Schedules.* New York: Catalyst, 1973. 15p.

This Catalyst position paper describes seven kinds of part-time employment designed to meet the needs and abilities of college-educated women who wish to maintain a career by working part-time, especially during early child-rearing years.

71.   Ford, John, and Isabella McTavish. *Job Sharing and Work Sharing: A Selected Bibliography.* Toronto: Ontario Ministry of Labour Library, 1980. 12p.

This bibliography includes citations only for books, government documents, periodical and newspaper articles pertaining to work sharing and job sharing.

72.   Frease, Michael, and Robert A. Zawacki. "Job Sharing: An Answer to Productivity Problems?" *Personnel Administrator* 24 (October 1979): 35-38+56.

The authors define job sharing, job pairing, and job splitting in addition to detailing both advantages and disadvantages of job sharing. They also include a list of professions engaging in job sharing. Bibliography.

73.   Friedman, Dana. "The Juggling Act." *Working Mother* 14 (September 1991): 41.

Friedman, co-president of the Families and Work Institute in New York City, answers a question on how to find the right person to share a job: begin with the personnel department (because it will know if other employees have inquired about part-time work); next, make a list of all your own job responsibilities and how these could be divided. When meeting prospective partners, examine how your work habits, experiences, and talents mesh with theirs.

74. Fryer, John. "Job-Split Splits Critics." *Times* (London), 14 November 1982, 59.

    In an effort to cut unemployment, the British government has initiated a job-splitting plan for which it offers some compensation. Critics, however, argue that job splitters will not be protected against unfair dismissal or be guaranteed unemployment benefits.

75. *General Bibliography on Job Sharing.* Palo Alto, CA: New Ways to Work, 1976. 16p.

    This bibliography contains government documents, books, magazine articles, and newspaper reports on part-time employment and job sharing.

76. Gibb-Clark, Margot. "Job Sharing: Good Outweighs Bad." *Globe and Mail* (Toronto), 26 July 1985, 7.

    Canadian employees are enjoying the benefits of job sharing. Market researchers, librarians, and insurance personnel find sharing beneficial to them. There are, however, situations in which job sharing does not work and where both employers and employees contribute to the failures.

77. Gilman, Robert. "Job Sharing is Good." *CoEvolution Quarterly* (Spring 1978): 86-90.

    Gilman explains why both employees and employers find job sharing advantageous, why it would benefit society, and why Americans are not doing it. He encourages those involved with job sharing to tell others of their experiences, thus informing workers and encouraging the use of more job-sharing opportunities.

78. Gilmore, Sue. "Job Sharing: Boon or Bane? Blessing or Barrier?" *Sacramento Union*, 20 July 1980, C3.

    While job sharing gets glowing reports from sharers themselves, there are those who question its validity. Labor unions are usually skeptical. Some workers feel management will use job sharing as a way of dangling leisure time before an employee or as a way of keeping women in subordinate positions by limiting the upward mobility of job sharers.

79. Goodhart, Philip, Sir. *Stand on Your Own Four Feet: A Study of Work Sharing and Job Splitting*. London: Bow Publications, 1982. 31p.

    Goodhart in this booklet encourages the British government to urge businesses to adopt job-sharing programs and to spread information about them. He feels a work-sharing plan will play a major role in alleviating the unemployment problems in Britain in addition to supporting the needs of women workers and prospective retirees. Instances of successful job-sharing arrangements are included.

80. Gould, Whitney. "Job Sharing: An Alternative to the 40-Hour Week." *Capital Times* (Madison, WI), 23 September 1976, 29.

    Gould reports on various positions in the State of Wisconsin that are being filled by two people under job-sharing agreements and why this work alternative has become acceptable.

81. Grady, Sharon. "One Job, Two Careers." *Working Woman* 6 (March 1981): 79-80+82+84+108.

    Grady points out the distinctions between part-time employment and job sharing, why employees and employers are supportive of job sharing, and why certain aspects of a job-sharing program, such as benefits, must be worked out by all concerned.

82. Gregory, Nona P., and Priscilla B. Schueck. "One Job, Two Contented Workers." *Voluntary Action Leadership* (Winter 1988): 7.

    This article continues a previous discussion (see item No. 9) on job sharing in the volunteer administration field. Associate directors of the Voluntary Action Center of the Lehigh Valley in Bethlehem, Pennsylvania, describe their responsibilities, the negative reactions they encountered, and how they share the duties of the position.

83. Griggs, Sue. *Job Sharing*. Toronto: Social Planning Council of Metropolitan Toronto, 1982. 14p.

    This booklet was prepared for a conference on work and the quality of family life that explored three new work models (work sabbaticals, work sharing, and job sharing). Definitions are given for each, with an expanded discussion on job sharing, including its advantages and disadvantages, successful experiences, and implications for the future. Bibliography.

84. Groom, Brian. "Discovering the Joys of Job Sharing." *Financial Times* (London), 15 October 1980, 15.

Employers who are reluctant to initiate alternative work patterns may find that the flexibility of job sharers and the increased chance of hiring experienced workers will outweigh many of the negative aspects of alternative staffing.

85. Grossmann, John. "Working in Tandem." *American Way* 15 (April 1982): 37+39+41+43+45+47.

Grossmann profiles several companies that have since the 1970s allowed their employees to job share. Shared jobs appeal to working mothers, retirees, students, and two-career couples as a way to "balance budgets, career and family concerns as well as the emotional need to work with a longing for free time." According to Grossmann, the role of film critic at the *New Yorker* magazine was divided by two women, each working six-months at a time.

86. *A Guide to Developing a Job Sharing Project.* Bethesda, MD: ERIC Document Reproduction Service, 1976. 78p. ED 134 798.

Designed for use in a workshop setting, this guide shows employees how to organize and promote part-time jobs. It includes a history, a glossary of terms, a model job-sharing project, examples of people who are sharing, and strategies for employer contact. Also included are exercises on job sharing, pairing, identifying employers, and role-playing interviews for the workshop participants as well as readers of the guide. Bibliography.

87. "A Guide to Job Sharing and Other Alternative Work Scheduling Patterns." *Stores* 63 (December 1981): 33.

In this article, Barney Olmsted, co-director of New Ways to Work in San Francisco, lists several ways for employers to introduce job sharing into their organizations.

88. Harriman, Ann. *The Work/Leisure Trade Off: Reduced Work Time for Managers and Professionals.* New York: Praeger, 1982. 184p.

This book contains a glossary defining various work-time options and includes several pages describing how job sharing can meet the needs of personnel interested in reduced work schedules. Various places where job sharing was, or is, taking place are detailed along with the activities of organizations such as Catalyst in New York City and New Ways to Work in San Francisco.

89. Harvey, David. "Job Sharing: What's in It for the Employer?" *Chief Executive* (May 1983): 9-10.

It can be argued that two chief job-sharing benefits—lower absenteeism and higher productivity—outweigh the disadvantages associated with job sharing. Specifications for the British government's grants to job-sharing employers are outlined in this article. Also included is a description of GEC Telecommunications' plan to employ job sharers.

90. Hatton, Jackie. "Happy Returns." *Woman and Home* (November 1987): 49+51+190.

Job sharing is an option for women who want to return to work. Hatton talks with three "returners," all of whom praise job sharing because it allows them to re-enter their chosen career field in addition to providing them time at home.

91. Hickman, Patricia, Tony Peckson, and Pat Willie. *A Study of Job Sharing in the Utah State Department of Social Services.* Salt Lake City: Office of Personnel Management, 1981. 21p.

This study reports on the research conducted to evaluate job sharing in the Utah State Department of Social Services. The research concentrated on three main topics: job satisfaction, life satisfaction, and partner relations. Preliminary interviews were conducted, questionnaires mailed, and the results analyzed. The conclusions showed no significant difference between job sharers and full-time workers concerning job satisfaction but revealed job sharers seem to be more satisfied with life than full-time workers. Good partner relations were found to be essential.

92. Hohn, Marcia D. *The Complete Guide to Job Sharing*. Andover, MA: M.D. Hohn, 1982. 75p. ERIC, ED 226 112.

    Beginning with an overview of job sharing, this illustrated booklet describes a job-sharing project in Massachusetts' Merrimack Valley where twelve professional women were recruited to participate in an eight-month demonstration project. Topics include identification of the jobs that were shared, goals and objectives, implementation of the project, and conclusions with recommendations. Samples of joint resumes are included. The final chapter covers job sharing as an alternative to layoffs.

93. *How to Split or Share Your Job*. San Francisco: New Ways to Work [1982]. 56p.

    Intended to help full-time employees reduce their work hours, this book describes how to restructure a job so that it can be split or shared. Also included are appendices covering a cost analysis, sample proposals, sample joint cover letters, joint resumes, and questions employers might ask in job-sharing interviews. Bibliography.

94. Hughes, Stephanie Downs. "Job Sharing--the Idea and the Practice." *News Bulletin* (Boston Chapter, Special Libraries Association) 42 (May/June 1976): 45-47.

    Hughes describes job sharing and job pairing, provides a typical hourly work schedule for two people sharing a job, and lists anticipated advantages for both employers and employees. Bibliography.

95. *Humanizing the Work Place: Quality of Work Life in Libraries*. Chicago: American Library Association, Office for Library Personnel Resources, 1983. 1 portfolio.

    Published as "Topics in Personnel" (kit number four), this portfolio contains copies of various articles on alternative work schedules and part-time employment, especially in libraries. Also included are several bibliographies that reference job-sharing articles.

96. *Indexed Bibliography on Alternative Work Schedules*. New York: Catalyst, 1988. 36p.

Articles and reports on various alternative work schedules--compressed workweek, flextime, telecommuting, job sharing, leaves of absence, part-time, temporary employees, work sharing, and others--are included in this bibliography.

97. *Interim Hearing on Flextime, Reduced Worktime and Job Sharing*. Sacramento: Joint Publications, 1986. 31p.

This document is the transcript of the August 24, 1986, hearing held by California's Senate Subcommittee on Women in the Workforce. It covers such questions as these: What is job sharing? Will job sharing help older workers make the transition to retirement? What has been done in California and throughout the nation? Speakers testifying are experts on the subject of alternative work time, including employees from New Ways to Work in San Francisco and the Sacramento Work Alternative Network in addition to job sharers themselves.

98. "Irish Congress of Trade Unions Adopts Policy on Job Sharing." *Work Times* 3 (Fall 1985): 1-2.

This article contains excerpts from the Irish Congress of Trade Unions' (ICTU) document on job sharing. The congress feels that job sharing will not create any new jobs and that it should not be used as an "alternative to the demand for an overall reduction in working hours for all workers." In addition, it does not want to see women forced into job-sharing arrangements.

99. Irwin, Victoria. "Job Sharing: A Flexible Solution." *Christian Science Monitor*, 24 January 1980, 17.

Workers are choosing the flexibility of sharing a job over a full-time position. Several states have passed legislation supporting job sharing, which is being taken advantage of by graduate students, married couples, mothers, and fathers.

100. Ivantcho, Barbara. *A Selected Annotated Bibliography on Work Time Options*. San Francisco: New Ways to Work, 1983. 35p.

Included in this bibliography are references on the following work-time options: permanent part-time, job sharing, phased retirement, leaves (sabbatical, educational, parental), and work sharing.

101. _____. *A Selected Annotated Bibliography on Work Time Options.* San Francisco: New Ways to Work, 1985. 42p.

   The author has included in this bibliography additional references to the same subjects that were in her 1983 bibliography. A new work-time option has been added-- voluntary reduced work-time programs.

102. _____. *A Selected Annotated Bibliography on Work Time Options.* San Francisco: New Ways to Work, 1989. 43p.

   This bibliography contains more references to the work-time options that were included in previous bibliographies prepared by Barbara Ivantcho. New topics include: annual hours programs and telecommuting, home-based work, and short-term assignment.

103. Jacob, Louise. "Job Sharing." *Employee Relations* 3 (1981): viii.

   Part-time work is often viewed as synonymous with low pay, low status, and temporary employment. Job sharing, on the other hand, is more closely associated with full-time work-- having status, security, and benefits. The London-based New Ways to Work (previously The Job Sharing Project) assists both employees and employers in establishing job-sharing positions.

104. Jennings, Nikki. "Conference on Job Sharing." *Essex* (England) *Chronicle,* 19 September 1986, 18.

   Researchers at the Essex Institute undertook a job-sharing study of 263 firms and held a conference to discuss their results. While only 18 percent of the businesses replied, they found 153 people (including 10 men) were job sharing in Southeast Essex, and 83 percent of the local government sample had a job-sharing scheme. More job-sharing opportunities exist in local government than in retail trade.

105. Jeune, Tracy. "Joys and Pitfalls of Job Sharing." *Times* (London), 12 September 1981, 21.

   Jeune describes the popularity of job sharing among certain types of workers (mothers, retirees, and those unable to work full-time because of health reasons). She further details financial pitfalls such as pension plans, unemployment benefits, and family income supplements that may not be available to those sharers in low-paying positions.

106. "Job Hunt Strategies for Part-Time Professionals." *Changing Times* 38 (July 1984): 62+64-65.

This article includes valuable tips for the person looking for a position to job share. Individuals should know what they want, develop a plan, and convince employers it will work.

107. "Job Sharing--A Growing Trend." *Canadian Industrial Relations and Personnel Developments* (10 November 1976): 818.

Business employers support job sharing because it reduces absenteeism and increases productivity. It may, however, be more expensive to train two people than one and they may need more supervision and equipment.

108. *Job Sharing: A Guide for Employers.* London: New Ways to Work, 1981. 26p.

This booklet lists and describes employers in the private, public, and nonprofit sector that have job-sharing programs available to their employees. It includes advantages to the employer, how to set up a program, costs involved, and benefits that may be statutory or negotiated.

109. *Job Sharing: A Manual for Sharing a Job, A Manual for Employers, A Manual for Bargaining Units.* Lansing, MI: Michigan Department of Labor, Bureau of Employment and Training, 1981. 28p. 34p. 40p.

Directed at potential sharers, the first manual gives background information and advantages, tells how to find a partner, and includes a sample of a joint proposal letter and joint resume. The second manual is written for the employer. It includes factors relating to increased cost-effectiveness, better job performance, and better use of the labor pool in addition to employer concerns such as cost issues, inconveniences, and the "steamroller effect." Benefits for, and concerns of, bargaining units are identified in the third manual. Also included are examples of work schedules, examples of governmental actions, and model projects relating to job sharing. Bibliography.

110.   "Job Sharing–A New Approach to Part-Time Work." In *Part-Time Work in Canada: Report of the Commission of Inquiry into Part-Time Work.* Ottawa: Labour Canada, 1983, pp. 173-186.

This chapter looks at job sharing in Canada, including its history, attitudes toward it, and reasons for it. Through the use of a questionnaire, the commission was able to obtain the views of 104 job sharers and 37 employers. Included are the advantages and disadvantages, how tasks are divided, communications, and pay benefits in addition to ways of establishing a job-sharing arrangement.

111.   "Job Sharing: A New Way to Work That Works!" *Current Consumer* 6 (October 1981): 18-19.

Splitting the responsibilities of a full-time job can reduce stress but job sharers point out that both individuals share the credit for jobs well done. Sharers must trust one another, be supportive, cooperative, and responsible.

112.   *Job Sharing: A Selected Bibliography.* London: New Ways to Work, 1988. 13p.

This annotated bibliography contains 22 book entries and 124 newspaper and magazine articles written in the 1980s. Most of the entries deal with job sharing in general, report on new developments, or feature interesting job sharers. All available items are cited and annotated individually elsewhere in this study.

113.   "Job-Sharing Agency to Build on Its Success." *Chelmsford* (England) *Weekly News*, 22 October 1987, 39.

Two women entrepreneurs establish a job-sharing agency–-Gemini Recruitment–-in Chelmsford. They wholeheartedly support job sharing and work with all types of personnel in setting up jobs. (See item No. 326 for a related article.)

114.   *The Job Sharing Alternative.* Hartford, CT: Permanent Commission on the Status of Women, 1985. 55p.

In response to an act passed in the Connecticut legislature, the Permanent Commission on the Status of Women was directed to make available to state employees and teachers materials on the subject of job sharing. This book is the result of their work. In addition to defining split-level employment, job pairing, job sharing, and job splitting, the text lists advantages and disadvantages and typical schedules for job sharers. Also included are case histories, a glossary, and guidelines. Bibliography.

115. "Job Sharing: An Attractive Option." *Management World* 13 (February 1984): 23-24.

While employees view job sharing as a means of reducing their hours in order to have more personal time, employers see the advantages of having a wider range of talent available to them.

116. "Job Sharing: An Effective Problem-Solving Tool." *Effective Manager* 5 (1982): 5-6.

This article gives examples of how job sharing can solve problems for managers concerned with absenteeism, layoffs, early retirement, and resignations.

117. *Job Sharing: An Introduction for Employers*. London: New Ways to Work, 1987. 4p.

Written for managers and employers investigating job sharing, this fact sheet answers several questions: Why do employers hire job sharers? What are the benefits? What types of jobs are shared? Which employers have adopted job sharing?

118. *Job Sharing: An Introductory Guide*. London: New Ways to Work, 1988. 32p.

This booklet is a general introduction to job sharing intended for employees and employers considering the possibilities of job sharing. It answers the following questions: Why do people share jobs? What kind of positions are shared? Who employs sharers and why? How does job sharing work? What kinds of questions do employers ask? Bibliography.

119. *Job Sharing: Analyzing the Cost*. San Francisco: New Ways to Work, 1981. 30p.

Designing a cost analysis by position and program is discussed in this book. A detailed worksheet is included for a cost analysis by position using sample figures for salary, benefits (statutory, compensatory, and supplementary), and indirect costs such as training and supervising. Bibliography.

120. *Job Sharing and Companies*. London: New Ways to Work, 1989. 8p.
   The need for new work patterns is discussed in this booklet along with how job sharing works and several examples of companies that have job-sharing alternatives available.

121. *Job Sharing and Voluntary Organizations*. London: New Ways to Work, 1983. 28p.
   This book reports on a conference sponsored jointly by New Ways to Work (London) and the National Council for Voluntary Organizations (London). A goal of the conference was to encourage voluntary and community organizations to consider the relevance of job sharing and to help promote it. Speakers discussed the practical implications of job sharing, the employer's view, job sharing in the voluntary sector, and the British government's job-splitting scheme.

122. *Job Sharing*. Brighton, England: Institute of Manpower Studies, 1982. 67p.
   Reporting on research conducted through interviews and a sample of respondents, this book looks at current prospects for the autonomous growth of part-time employment, the role of labor costs in stimulating or inhibiting this growth, and how a financial subsidy for job sharing might increase the possibilities for part-time work in England. Included is a summary of the major findings of the research, developments in the use of part-time labor, potential for job sharing, implementing job-sharing programs, how to make a job-sharing subsidy work, and a draft directive on part-time workers' rights. Bibliography.

123. "Job Sharing: Can Two Work as Cheaply as One?" *Manitoba Business* 41 (November 1983): 25-26.
   Canadian employers may pay more unemployment insurance for job sharers if they are both in a high-income bracket. Increased productivity, however, often offsets higher administrative costs and extra time required for training.

124. "Job Sharing Catches On." *Business Week* (25 October 1976): E112.

   A few U.S. businesses and state and city governments are beginning to adopt job-sharing programs. The California city of Palo Alto offers job sharing in the office of city manager. In the same city, the Hudson Publishing Company accepted the application and hired two potential job sharers because "together they simply offered a lot more than any single applicant."

125. "Job Sharing." *Co-op Scan* (York University) (October 1981): unnumbered.

   Job sharing is defined and described as a white-collar phenomenon that has not been made available to the blue-collar workforce.

126. *Job Sharing: Developing a Program.* San Francisco: New Ways to Work, 1980. 23p.

   Written for the personnel administrator or manager, this handbook gives general guidelines for developing a job-sharing program, converting a full-time position to a shared one, and creating support for the program by increasing participation. Questions (and answers) most frequently asked are also given.

127. *Job Sharing: Employment Rights and Conditions.* Rev. ed. London: New Ways to Work, 1988. 19p.

   Included in this booklet are items on a job-sharing contract that should be reviewed and agreed upon by both employer and employee. These items include the following: hours of work, rate of pay, overtime pay, sick pay, maternity/paternity leave, pensions, promotion, training, overlap time, covering for a partner, one partner leaving, unemployment, and returning to full-time work.

128. "Job Sharing." *Equal Opportunities Review* 16 (November/ December 1987): 12-16.

   Job sharing is explained in this article as well as its pros and cons, the types of positions that can be shared, and how it works (recruitment, selection, registration, statutory rights, hours, pay, holidays, insurance, training, promotion, and resignation).

129. *Job Sharing: Final Report of a CETA Funded Pilot Project.* Palo
      Alto, CA: New Ways to Work, 1977. 54p.

      This report describes a job-sharing pilot project that was
      funded by the Comprehensive Employment and Training Act
      (CETA). The whole issue of job sharing was investigated,
      workshops were held for prospective clients (sharers) and
      employers (after they were identified), and a talent bank was
      established for employees wishing to find partners. The staff of
      New Ways to Work developed many of the workshop materials
      (glossary, application letter, resume, and bibliography). They
      also made plans to continue their work of "selling" the concept
      of job sharing to employers. Bibliography.

130. "Job Sharing Has Growing Appeal for Workers Seeking
      Alternatives to Traditional Employment Patterns." *World of
      Work Report* 4 (May 1979): 35-36.

      This article reports on a survey of job sharers conducted by
      Gretl Meier and published under the title—*Job Sharing: A New
      Pattern for Quality of Work and Life* (see item No. 204). Also
      included are definitions of horizontal and vertical job sharing.

131. "Job Sharing Helps Working Mothers but Has Some
      Drawbacks." *Wall Street Journal,* 30 July 1985, E1.

      While some working mothers enjoy job sharing, others say
      it can put one's career on hold or create a work load that is more
      than one person can handle on a shared basis.

132. *Job Sharing: How to Incorporate Sharers into the Organization.*
      San Francisco: New Ways to Work, 1980. 25p.

      This handbook contains pages on recruiting, interviewing,
      redesigning jobs, implementing, and evaluating. Sample
      advertisements, work schedules, and the division of
      duties/responsibilities are also included.

133. *Job Sharing: Improving the Quality and Availability of Part-
      Time Work.* Manchester, England: Equal Opportunities
      Commission, 1981. 33p.

      Job sharing in the United Kingdom and the United States is
      discussed in this book. Identification of job-sharing schemes,
      individual arrangements, statutory rights, negotiated and con-

tributed benefits as well as potential advantages and drawbacks for both employees and employers are outlined. Bibliography.

134. "Job Sharing." In *Alternative Work Schedules: Selecting, Implementing, and Evaluating*, by Simcha Ronen. Homewood, IL: Dow Jones-Irwin, 1984, pp. 161-192.

In this chapter, the author presents a comprehensive view of job sharing, including various definitions, profiles of job sharers, pilot programs in both the public and private sectors, and implications (positive and negative) for employees and employers. Several companies (including TRW Vidar, Black & Decker, and Hewlett-Packard) and their job-sharing programs are detailed. Bibliography.

135. "Job Sharing." In *Flexible Work Arrangements: Establishing Options for Managers and Professionals*. New York: Catalyst, 1989, pp. 56-82.

Catalyst, a national organization that works with corporations to promote the development of women's careers and leadership abilities, believes "flexibility will be the hallmark of the 1990s." Job sharing was one type of flexible work arrangement that Catalyst researchers investigated. The chapter on job sharing includes background information, issues for supervisors and job sharers, types of jobs shared, and impact on career development as well as information on job-sharing arrangements in seven companies.

136. "Job Sharing." In *Goodbye, 9 to 5*, by Michel Syrett. London: New Opportunity Press, 1985, pp. 75-81.

Syrett writes that job sharing offers an opportunity to overcome the disadvantages (low pay and few prospects for promotion or additional training) of traditional part-time employment. He includes the advantages and disadvantages of job sharing as well as ways of finding a partner and an employer.

137. "Job Sharing." In *Negotiating Shorter Working Hours*, by Alastair Evans and Stephen Palmer. London: Macmillan, 1985, pp. 57-64.

Included here is a description of the British government's job-splitting scheme, the advantages and disadvantages of job sharing, as well as various working patterns, such as the split day, split week, alternate week, or no fixed schedule--all of which may be utilized by job sharers.

138. *Job Sharing in the London Boroughs*. Rev. ed. London: New Ways to Work, 1987. 4p.

Boroughs within London that have formal job-sharing policies are listed alphabetically in this pamphlet. Each entry includes a short policy description. Additional statements identify what kind of jobs are shared, pension benefits, and how to find a job to share.

139. "Job Sharing in the Public Sector." *MITC Reporter* (Midwest Intergovernmental Training Committee, Bloomington, IN) 2 (November 1979): whole issue.

This issue of the *MITC Reporter* focuses on job sharing by reviewing Wisconsin's Project JOIN (Job Options and Innovations), which began in June 1976. Tables are given showing statistics on participants and their employment rights and benefits. Examples of questions that arose when tasks were divided are included as well as solutions to problems encountered by sharers.

140. "Job Sharing." *Inc.* 10 (May 1988): 130.

This pictorial featuring a map of the United States divides the country into five areas that show the percentage of companies in each area that have job sharing. The Midwest and Great Lakes regions have the largest percentages.

141. "Job Sharing: Is It the Way to Go?" *Personal Report for the Executive* 13 (15 November 1987): 2-3.

Guidelines are presented here for the manager who is considering the use of job sharing as a means of solving staffing needs. They include the following: evaluating the incumbent, interviewing, handling communication, prorating salary benefits, preparing other employees, and setting a trial period.

142. "Job Sharing: Labour Pains." *Economist* 282 (20 March 1982): 75+77.

Holland businessmen say job sharing works for women in office positions but not for men in blue-collar factory jobs. Married men in part-time positions feel inadequate bringing home a partial paycheck and fellow full-time workers resent the employee's part-time status.

143. *Job Sharing.* London: Work Research Unit, 1985. 8p.

These pages consist of a bibliography of sixty-two items (books and periodical articles) published in the late 1970s and early 1980s. Items are repeated in this bibliography.

144. *Job Sharing.* Rev. ed. San Francisco: New Ways to Work, 1982. 11p.

This handbook for employers is a reprint in part of a booklet published in 1980 under the same title (see item No. 145 below).

145. *Job Sharing.* San Francisco: New Ways to Work, 1980. 11p. ERIC, ED 197 087.

Due to an increase in workers' desires for more flexible employment arrangements, job sharing has risen in popularity. This pamphlet explains what job sharing is and how it works, the kinds of jobs that can be shared, and how an organization can benefit in addition to potential problems. An example of a daily work schedule is also illustrated.

146. "Job Sharing." *Spare Rib* (June 1978): 32-33.

Interest in job sharing is found not only among employees but also among employers, unions, and governmental agencies. This article describes several positions in which job sharers are employed. The overwhelming advantage seen by these employees is the flexibility inherent in job sharing.

147. "Job Sharing: Where One-Half Plus One-Half Equals More Than One." In *Of Cradles and Careers: A Guide to Reshaping Your Job to Include a Baby in Your Life*, by Kaye Lowman. Franklin Park, IL: La Leche League International, 1984, pp. 49-69.

This chapter contains tips on how to choose a job-sharing partner, how to deal with problems, how to initiate a program, and how to present a written proposal. Also included is a section on the popularity of job sharing among teachers, with particular mention of sharing in the Schaumburg, Illinois, Township School District.

148. *Jobshare: How It Works for Employers.* Birmingham, England: Employment Department, 1989. 6p.

The Employment Department in Birmingham, England, explains in this promotional booklet how job sharing works, who is using it and why, in addition to telling how a prospective sharer applies.

149. "The Joys of Job Sharing." *Human Behavior* 5 (November 1976): 36.

New Ways to Work in Palo Alto, California, offers workshops and counseling services to employees wishing alternatives (job sharing is but one) to traditional work patterns.

150. Kahne, Hilda. *Reconceiving Part-Time Work: New Perspectives for Older Workers and Women.* Totowa, NJ: Rowman & Allanheld, 1985. 180p.

This book contains several pages describing the fringe benefits of job sharing, its administrative and supervisory costs, jobs suitable for sharing, and the prevalence of jobs that are shared. Bibliography.

151. Kalvelage, Joan, Patricia A. Schmuck, and Jane Arends. "Reductions in Force and Affirmative Action." *Educational Economics* 3 (January/February 1978): 12-14+23.

Coordination, communication, and interdependence are necessary for an effective job-sharing arrangement. This article includes the advantages of both permanent part-time work and job sharing as well as identifying unsolved problems articulated by union leaders.

152. Kane, Ros. "New Ways to Work." *London Voluntary News* (January 1982): 11.

In 1977 a small group of London community workers formed an organization to campaign for more flexible work schedules. This group, originally known as the Job Sharing

Project, later changed its name to New Ways to Work and has been influential in establishing and supporting job-sharing arrangements.

153. Karpf, Anne. "Part-Time Prejudice." *Company* (London) (August 1981): 76-77+81-83.

Part-time work has historically carried negative connotations and has never enjoyed the benefits associated with full-time employment. Job sharing may have the potential to improve the quality of part-time work both for employees and employers. Several workers describe why and how job sharing became, and continues to be, an important change in their work life.

154. Katzman, Marvin Stewart. "Alternative Work Patterns: A Predictive Model for Organizations in the United States." D.B.A. thesis, George Washington University, 1981. 225p.

Katzman's dissertation looks at management's view of alternative work patterns. He analyzed survey responses from 214 organizations that were using some type of alternative work pattern (flexible working hours, job sharing, permanent part-time work, and the compressed workweek). He concludes with a predictive model to assist organizations in determining the feasibility of alternative work patterns. Bibliography.

155. Keegan, Bridget, and Betsy Barker. "Gizza Job Share." *New Society* 78 (12 December 1986): iii.

Voluntary organizations in the London boroughs have been very supportive of job sharing because both the organizations and the workers benefit from the arrangement.

156. Kennedy, Joyce Lain. "Job Sharing Is Gaining Ground." *Blade* (Toledo, OH), 23 April 1978, E8.

Kennedy responds to a question on job sharing in her careers column by giving a definition, listing examples of professions engaged in job sharing, and identifying some of its benefits.

157. _____. "Job Sharing Offers Time, Flexibility." *Chicago Sun Times*, 30 April 1978, 96.
     Cited above as item No. 156.

158. Kiester, Sally Valente. "Job Sharing--A Paycheck and Spare Time, Too." *Chicago Sun Times*, 30 November 1980, *Parade Magazine* 36+39+41.
     The most surprising information in this article is that a split-week schedule is not always the norm for job sharers. Kiester describes one couple who divides a job on a 25-to-75 percent basis and other couples who alternate working a week, three months, and six months at a time.

159. Kirshner, Abraham. "Job Sharing." *Canadian Forum* 64 (March 1985): 28-29+41.
     In this article the author proposes a solution to mandatory job sharing (often referred to as work sharing). Specifically, voluntary job sharing occurs when workers elect to give up half their salary by working half-time. This allows them free time for leisure, educational pursuits, or family obligations.

160. Knickerbocker, Brad. "Job Sharing Catches On." *Christian Science Monitor*, 13 December 1976, 2.
     Government agencies may have accepted job sharing more readily than businesses but it is increasing in corporations. Employers are discovering it is good for their business.

161. Koblinsky, Sally A., and Kathleen F. Mikitka. "Job Sharing: A Part-Time Career for a Fuller Life." *Journal of Home Economics* 76 (Winter 1984): 6-10+19.
     This article includes a description of job sharing and why it is of interest to home economists and others. Also described are types of people most likely to become job sharers and what they will face in terms of advantages and disadvantages. Prospective job sharers will also find useful a plan for securing a shared position. Bibliography.

162. Korpivaara, Ari. "Will Men 'Legitimize' Part-Time Work?" *Ms* 9 (May 1981): 37-38+40.

Job sharing can be ideal for men who wish to help in caring for their children, to pursue second careers, or to phase into retirement. On the other hand, the male part-timer is often viewed by bosses and co-workers as someone who is not serious about his work.

163. Kuenning, Shelley, and Penny Jensen. *Job Sharing: How to Get a Full-Time Salary in a Part-Time Job.* Manassas, VA: Ranger Publications, 1982. 31p.

This is a guide for the woman who wants to go back to work via job sharing. Included are chapters on finding a suitable partner, writing a resume, drafting a job-sharing proposal, and scheduling the interview in addition to tips for a successful interview.

164. "Labor Softening on Job Sharing." *Vancouver Sun,* 4 October 1982, A2.

Organized labor in Canada is accepting contracts for job sharing among teachers and nurses. Job sharing must, however, be differentiated from work sharing.

165. Labreche, Julianne. "Two Can Work as Cheaply as One." *Financial Post Magazine* 75 (31 October 1981): 22+24+26.

Labreche describes why both Canadian women and men are finding job sharing attractive and how it is increasing the possibilities of part-time work for professionals. This article includes many examples of where job sharing is occurring in Canada.

166. Lantin, Barbara. "When Two-Timing Is Good News for Everyone." *Jewish Chronicle,* 6 November 1987, 13.

London-area women workers describe why job sharing works for them. One couple divides work on a product basis. Although they do not have significant overlap, either one can pick up the other's projects if necessary. A disadvantage is that sharers often work longer hours than called for in the split arrangement.

167. Laqueur, Maria. *Flexible Work Options: A Selected Bibliography*. Falls Church, VA: Association of Part-Time Professionals, 1990. 44p.

   This bibliography contains 468 citations on flexible work options including job sharing, part-time employment, telecommuting, flextime, home-based work, phased retirement, and work sharing. It contains a keyword and organization index. Approximately 60 of the entries deal with the topic of job sharing.

168. Laursen, Irene. "Alternate Work Patterns–A Selective Bibliography." *News Bulletin* (Boston Chapter, Special Libraries Association) 42 (May/June 1976): 55-59.

   This annotated bibliography includes ten citations on job sharing (listed separately in this work) and part-time employment. The other topics are flextime, the four-day workweek, and volunteering.

169. Lazer, Robert I. "Job Sharing as a Pattern for Permanent Part-Time Work." *Conference Board Record* 12 (October 1975): 57-61.

   Flexibility in work scheduling is a major selling point for proponents of job sharing. The author examines several pros and cons of the issue and reiterates two important attributes job sharers must possess in addition to flexibility: the ability to communicate and cooperate. Also included is a chart showing various work schedules that could be utilized by two people sharing a workweek.

170. Lee, Patricia. *The Complete Guide to Job Sharing*. New York: Walker, 1983. 136p.

   Written as a guide to introduce prospective job sharers and employers to the concept of job sharing, this book identifies both the pros and cons of the issue. It delves into the work environment, job descriptions, finding a partner, time schedules, fringe benefits, communication tools, and joint resumes/ interviews. Also included are sample forms and a listing of professional associations/organizations offering support to job sharers and employers. Bibliography.

171. _____. "Job Sharing." *Secretary* 44 (January 1984): 22.

Job sharing is one way to meet the demand for more flexible employment patterns and work schedules. This article--excerpted from the author's *The Complete Guide to Job Sharing* (see item No. 170 above)--includes a detailed list of things a prospective sharer needs in order to develop a plan.

172. Leib, Jeffrey. "Flexible Work Arrangements Burgeoning." *Denver Post*, 30 October 1989, C1.

Leib reports that more companies than before are allowing their employees to choose flexible work schedules. He says this helps companies to recruit and retain the best employees. He also reports that Catalyst, a research organization interested in workplace issues, found that "job sharers take shorter maternity leaves and have smoother returns to work."

173. Leighton, Patricia. "Job Sharing--Opportunities or Headaches?" *Employee Relations* 8 (1986): 27-31.

Leighton discusses changes (job sharing) in the United Kingdom labor market, describes who are job sharers, reports on establishing a shared position, and analyzes job sharing from a legal viewpoint. Bibliography.

174. _____. "Job Sharing--Some Issues for Labour Law." *Industrial Law Journal* 15 (September 1986): 173-182.

The author cites several court cases to point out problems with, and controversies surrounding, the job-share employment contract in the United Kingdom. She distinguishes job sharing from the British government's job-splitting scheme and notes differences between "core" and "peripheral" employees as related to the job-sharing issue and labor laws that affect employment rights and benefits of workers.

175. _____. "Progress and Pitfalls of Job Sharing." *Social and Labour Bulletin* (March 1987): 5-9.

This article is an excerpt from "Job Sharing--Opportunities or Headaches?" (see item No. 173 above).

176. _____. "Responses to Vulnerability: The Example of Job Sharing." *Employee Relations* 9 (1987): 49-59.

Leighton explores ways in which economic and legal vulnerability of workers can be alleviated or cured. If job sharing is to provide workers protection from vulnerability, care must be taken in establishing the shared arrangement so that it contributes to improving the working conditions of employees and ensures that workers are satisfied. Bibliography.

177. _____. "Whatever Happened to Job Splitting?" *Manpower Policy and Practice* (Winter 1986): 4-5.

The differences between job sharing and job splitting are explained in this article in addition to why the British government's job-splitting scheme ran into opposition and has not been used effectively.

178. Leighton, Patricia, and Catherine Rayner. *Job Sharing in South-East Essex*. Chelmsford, England: Essex Institute of Higher Education, Employment Relations Research Centre, 1986. 52p.

Leighton and Rayner studied via the use of two questionnaires (management and trade union) the issues of job sharing in Southeast Essex. This research concentrated on people responsible for managing, supporting, and negotiating job-sharing programs rather than on-the-job sharers themselves. The management sample was divided into four parts: manufacturing, public sector, retail, and other. The trade union sample was comprised of both private and public sectors, including teaching and non-teaching unions. Bibliography.

179. Leighton, Patricia, and Marlene Winfield. *Does Job Sharing Work? Case Studies & Practical Guide*. London: Industrial Society; Chelmsford: Essex Institute of Higher Education, 1988. 51p.

This book is the result of research performed on seven in-depth case studies of job sharing in different work environments. People interviewed included these: the sharers themselves, their managers, colleagues (some were supervised by the sharers), union representatives, and personnel officers. For every case, the book details the origins of the job-sharing arrangement, the work demands, and what is involved in the job-sharing position. Other chapters include perceived gains and/or losses to the organization in addition to managerial issues that arise when job sharing is implemented. The conclusion describes the broader context of job sharing and provides a strategy for introducing and managing shared positions.

180. Leighton, Patricia, and Michel Syrett. *New Work Patterns: Putting Policy into Practice*. London: Pitman, 1989. 247p.

The purpose of this book is to provide practical information to employers about new work patterns and to provide guidance in choosing options that will meet the flexibility needs of both employees and management. The index contains thirty entries under job sharing, including advertising, contracts, management objectives, overtime, pension rights, preparation for job sharing, promotions, and trade unions. Chapter bibliographies.

181. Leonard, Dorothy. "Job Sharing--A Problem Halved." *My Weekly* (Scotland), 20 March 1982, 10-12.

Scottish female workers describe why job sharing works well for them. It allows them the benefit of working part-time as well as the luxury of more free time at home with their husbands and children.

182. Levine, Karen. "Flextime--It Works!" *Parents* 65 (September 1990): 170+172-174.

Levine defines job sharing as one of the "trends toward flexibility in the workplace." She gives information on job sharing at Steelcase, an office furniture manufacturer in Grand Rapids, Michigan, and describes why two academic advisers for Regents College in Albany, New York, decided job sharing was best for them after a position was expanded to allow three women to share two jobs.

183. Levitt, Irene S. "Guidelines for Job Sharing: An Alternative Work Option." *Library Personnel News* 1 (Fall 1987): 27.

These guidelines define paired job, shared job, split-level job, and split-location. Also included are a list of advantages for both employers and employees and an outline of a typical work schedule. Bibliography.

184. Libman, Joan. "Job Sharing." *Good Housekeeping* 188 (June 1979): 62+64+66+68+70.

The position of personnel representative at TRW Vidar, a California-based telecommunications firm, is shared by two women who were both previously working full-time in the personnel department. They have found it necessary to overlap some work time. They feel committed to each other as well as the job and they intend to work for a promotion together.

185. Lindorff, Dave. "Job Sharing." *Soho News*, 8 October 1980, 57.

Job sharing can be a way for people to have more control over their working lives even though some benefits (retirement and health) may be lost. While not all employers are receptive to the idea, more are becoming convinced.

186. Linscott, Judy. "Job Sharing: A New Career Choice." *Daily News* (New York), 18 November 1980, 37.

Job-sharing partners are dedicated to their job and do not view it as part-time in the traditional sense. They expect to get called on their days off and to rearrange their schedules to handle extra work or emergencies.

187. Lipovenko, Dorothy. "Job Sharing Favored by Working Mothers." *Globe and Mail* (Toronto), 17 January 1980, T10.

Some employers are hesitant to allow job sharing because it means they must increase their payroll contributions. To help solve this problem, the Toronto School Board decided to make job-sharing employees pay a portion of their benefits. Working mothers who enjoy the advantages of job sharing do not mind these extra costs.

188. Long, Marion C., and Susan W. Post. *State Alternative Work Schedule Manual*. Washington, DC: National Council for Alternative Work Patterns, 1981. 102p.

An alphabetical listing by state, this reference book summarizes the types of alternative work programs (flextime, compressed workweeks, permanent part-time, job sharing, transition retirement, and voluntary time-income tradeoffs) used by various agencies within each state.

189. Long, Richard J. "Patterns of Workplace Innovation in Canada." *Industrial Relations* 44 (Autumn 1989): 805-824.

This article reports on the results of a survey of Canadian organizations that were queried about their use of several types of workplace innovations--one of which was job sharing. Results showed job sharing to be very popular in 1982 and 1983. However, the author expressed concern over whether job sharing was being defined the same by all respondents. Some may have confused it with work sharing.

190. Lussier, Robert N. "Should Your Organization Use Job Sharing?" *Supervision* 51 (April 1990): 9-12.

After assessing organizational and employee needs as well as the advantages and disadvantages of job sharing, managers may wish to use job sharing to solve staffing problems. Lussier suggests ways in which job-sharing programs can be implemented.

191. Macaskill, Hilary. "Fair Shares for Two." *Observer* (London), 13 August 1978, Living [Section] 23.

Two workers (one female and one male) propose job sharing to the North Kensington Law Centre. Their proposal included the argument that the centre would be getting two minds for the price of one in addition to the experience and contacts each had. The centre accepted the proposal and the sharers have proven themselves to be invaluable. Both agree they probably could not afford to work part-time if their spouses did not earn a good wage.

192. MacDonald, Charlotte. "Job Sharing: Part-time Work with Full-Time Potential." *Woman's Day* (28 June 1977): 32+112.

Editorial assistants for a publishing firm share a position in Los Altos, California. It is the author's opinion that almost any job can be shared with the exception of those that require a great deal of travel, training, supervising, or decision making. If a job is advertised as a single position, it is up to the prospective sharers to convince the hiring personnel to accept them as a team.

193. Main, Jeremy. "Good Jobs Go Part-Time." *Money* 6 (October 1977): 80-86.

Job sharing is viewed as a way of upgrading and increasing part-time positions. Businesses, government offices, and educational institutions see the benefits in hiring two people instead of one. Married art professors share a teaching position at Grinnell College in Iowa.

194. Males, Carolyn, and Julie Raskin. "Why Not Share Your Job?" *Cosmopolitan* 192 (March 1982): 195+203-205+315.

Rigid rules for job sharing do not exist. After finding a partner and securing a position, it is up to the partners to make it work. It will be necessary to organize and plan for communication in addition to planning the division of salary and benefits. However, the key issue in a successful job-sharing arrangement appears to be flexibility.

195. Martin, Dale. "Job Sharing: A New Reality in the Workplace." *San Mateo (CA) Times*, 17 December 1984, B1.

Job sharing is a way for many professionals--school teachers, city managers, and magazine photographers--to combine a career with more free time at home.

196. Mattis, Mary C. "New Forms of Flexible Work Arrangements for Managers and Professionals: Myths and Realities." *Human Resource Planning* 13 (1990): 133-146.

This article summarizes a research project undertaken by Catalyst, the business women's research and advisory organization, to examine the flexibility of work arrangements that are available to professional and managerial employees. Job sharing and its levels of responsibility (shared, divided, or unrelated) are described as well as several commonly held myths about flexible work arrangements. The research, which consisted of telephone and personal interviews, uncovered the myths; the reality of the situation is detailed.

197. McHenry, Susan, and Linda Lee Small. "Does Part-Time Pay Off?" *Ms* 17 (March 1989): 88-94.

The authors give several examples of women working part-time and discuss why flexible work arrangements such as job sharing and part-time positions are viewed by several as a way of balancing work schedules and free time. They also point out, however, that part-time may mean no benefits and lower salaries.

198. McKendrick, Joseph E., Jr. "Stretching Time in '89." *Management World* 18 (July/August 1989): 10-11.

Reporting on a survey conducted by the Administrative Management Society, McKendrick states that employers with job sharing were up slightly over the previous year--from 8 percent to 9 percent with another 2 percent considering job-sharing plans.

199. McLaughlin, Paul. "Double Duty." *Canadian Business* 62 (April 1989): 115-116.

This article presents a hypothetical case--two salespeople want to share a position and present the idea to their boss who is skeptical and asks for advice. Both an expert in industrial relations and a previous job sharer offer their advice and opinions on job sharing.

200. McLoughlin, Jane. "Two to a Job." *Guardian* (London), 27 May 1980, 8.

McLoughlin begins by describing two launderette workers who split a single full-time job even though they do not get along very well on a personal level. She also describes the outlook for part-time employment in general in England, including attitudes of the trade unions.

201. Meade, Marion. "Back to Work? Go on Your Own Terms." *McCall's* 98 (July 1971): 46.

A New York City employment agency, Newtime, and a national nonprofit organization, Catalyst, both work toward employment for women who want part-time and flexible work schedules.

202. Meade-King, Maggy. "Two into One Will Go." *Guardian* (London), 27 June 1985, 9.

The author points out that traditional work schedules are arranged for the male breadwinner and that females who wish to work part-time are often stuck in low paying, low-status, no-security positions. However, job sharing a full-time position allows for many advantages the part-timer does not enjoy.

203. Meager, Nigel, and James Buchan. *Job Sharing and Job Splitting: Employer Attitudes.* Brighton, England: Institute of Manpower Studies, 1988. 99p.

The authors examine British employers' attitudes toward job sharing to see whether changes have occurred since an earlier study compiled in 1982 (see item No. 122). The findings are given under chapter topics that include these: use of part-time work, nature and extent of job sharing/job splitting, advantages and disadvantages, ways to implement programs, and the job-share scheme. Bibliography.

204. Meier, Gretl S. *Job Sharing: A New Pattern for Quality of Work and Life.* Kalamazoo, MI: W.E. Upjohn Institute for Employment Research, 1978. 187p.

Meier begins her book with the evolution of job sharing and then describes a survey she conducted in order to identify the type of people choosing job sharing. Meier surveyed 238 job sharers (teachers, administrators, ministers, counselors, social workers, and researchers). Included in this book are many tables that profile the sharers' views, attitudes, problems, and benefits. Also included are partnership profiles that quote many of the job sharers, their supervisors, and co-workers whom Meier interviewed. Bibliography.

205. _____. "Shared Job Project in California Stimulates Labor and Management Interest." *World of Work Report* 1 (September 1976): 7.

New Ways to Work, located in Palo Alto, California, has been responsible for a pilot project—initially funded by the Comprehensive Employment and Training Act—designed to establish shared jobs. New Ways to Work acts as a consultant with employers in establishing job-sharing programs and hiring part-timers interested in sharing.

206. Meives, Susan Fritch. "Part-Time Work: A Multiperspective Analysis." Ph.D. diss., University of Wisconsin, Madison, 1979. 286p.

Project JOIN (Job Options and Innovations) began in 1976 when the State of Wisconsin received a federal grant to establish part-time work and job sharing within the state civil service system. For her doctoral thesis, Meives studied three groups: job sharers employed for Project JOIN, applicants who were not hired for Project JOIN, and full-time workers in jobs comparable to the JOIN positions. Appendices and tables as well as text explain the impact of Project JOIN, job satisfaction among workers, preference for full-time or part-time work, and the employers' perspectives. Bibliography.

207. Merkin, Ann. "Job Sharing." *Women's Work* 4 (March/April 1978): 19-22+18.

Students, parents, handicapped workers, and older laborers can profit from a shorter workweek. Since part-time work often has no benefits (vacation, sick leave, insurance), workers are more interested in job sharing because it offers a "sharing" of all the benefits included in a full-time position. Employers see disadvantages in that fixed costs based on the number of employees increase with job sharing and unemployment contributions and Social Security taxes may be higher for a job-sharing team than a single worker.

208. Merriam, Elizabeth B. "Job Sharing: Successful Program for Permanent Professional Employees." *Wisconsin Library Bulletin* 75 (May-June 1979): 105-106.

Definitions for job sharing (or splitting), job pairing, and split-level employment arc included in this article. Statements are given by various people in job-sharing positions and the Wisconsin job-sharing endeavor--Project JOIN (Job Options and Innovations) is discussed.

209. Miller, Darla. "Divided Jobs May Conquer the Workplace." *San Jose* (CA) *Mercury*, 1 July 1981, C1+C3.

Women sharing various positions in California comment on why and how job sharing works for them. Nurses at the Stanford Medical Center, assistant deans at Stanford University, and personnel assistants at TRW Vidar all report on the advantages of job sharing.

210.   Miller, Leona. "Job Sharing: A Human Resource Alternative."
       M.B.A. thesis, New York Institute of Technology, 1985. 84p.
           This thesis is a limited overview of job sharing, including its
       advantages and disadvantages. Positive reactions of employees
       are given in addition to negative reactions of management.
       Bibliography.

211.   Miller, Margo. "How Workers Share a Job." *Boston Globe*, 6
       February 1981, 45-46.
           Two Andover, Massachusetts, women established the
       Merrimack Valley Job Sharing Project because they both wanted
       to work part-time and were having difficulty finding positions.
       They worked with both employees and prospective employers to
       set up shared positions.

212.   Miller, Rhonda. "Job Sharing: Two for One." *Tidewater
       Virginian* (October 1984): 73-76.
           Although job sharing exists in the State of Virginia, it has
       not caught on to a great extent. The three largest employers in
       the state do not have shared positions, in part because their
       employees have not requested it. Employers often cite extra
       supervision as a disadvantage of job sharing.

213.   Moncreiff, Ted, and Laurel Adams. "Companies Vary in Aid to
       Parents." *USA Today*, 14 March 1989, B4.
           USA Today reporters polled eleven large companies to find
       out what family-related benefits (day care, flextime, parental
       leaves, sabbaticals, working at home, and job sharing) they
       offered their employees. Flextime and parental leave had the
       most support. Job sharing was offered by Allstate and NCNB (a
       bank holding company). Others (Apple, Gannett, and Polaroid)
       said it was left to the manager's discretion and Merck said job
       sharing was experimental.

214.   Montague, Anne. "The Job Share Market." *She* (London)
       (August 1986): 62-65.
           While the majority of job sharers are women, married
       couples also benefit from job sharing. The author interviewed
       two married couples: journalists at one of London's newspapers,
       The Financial Times, and religious instructors at the University

of Lancaster. She also talked with two women sharing the position of children's librarian at Sheffield Central Library.

215. _____. "Job Sharing." *Woman's Own* (20 November 1982): 16-17.

Montague interviewed job sharers in several London businesses. All reported the greatest advantage of sharing was job flexibility. The author describes two organizations (GEC Telecommunications and West Midlands County Council) that are offering job sharing to unemployed youth. Also included is a listing with addresses of job-sharing groups ready to advise people about part-time opportunities.

216. Morris, Roz. "Part-Time Job, Full-Time Rewards." *Options* (April 1988): 125-126+128.

Job sharing is one part-time working option that is meeting the needs of several British workers. Morris talks with part-timers who successfully combine careers with free time for other activities.

217. Most, Bruce W. "The Job Sharers: Two Workers for the Price of One." *Kiwanis* 66 (May 1981): 19-21+44.

Further educational pursuits, leisure activities, and co-parenting are competing with time on the job. As a result, more workers are asking for flexible work arrangements even if their request is met with resistance. In most cases, it is the responsibility of the workers to suggest job sharing and then to prove they can make it work.

218. Mungall, Constance. "Part-Time Jobs: As Good as Full-Time, Only Shorter?" *Chatelaine* 50 (January 1977): 37+51+55-56.

Several patterns for permanent part-time positions are described in this article. These include the following: job pairing, job sharing, split-level, split-location, straight part-time, and consultant or specialist. Examples are included of women and men who are balancing part-time employment with more time at home.

219. Myers, Nell. "Sharing Job—And More." *Morning Star* (London), 13 July 1982, 4.

The London-based National Council for Civil Liberties through its Women's Rights Unit has actively campaigned for equal rights for women who prefer part-time employment.

220.   Newstrom, John W., and Jon L. Pierce. "Alternative Work Schedules: The State of the Art." *Personnel Administrator* 24 (October 1979): 19-23.

Definitions and descriptions of job sharing and job splitting are included in this general article on alternative work schedules.

221.   Nollen, Stanley D. *New Work Schedules in Practice: Managing Time in a Changing Society.* New York: Van Nostrand Reinhold, 1982. 281p.

Nollen, with the help of Gretl Meier, describes job sharing as a work alternative that includes advantages of both part-time and full-time employment. A hypothetical case of a large manufacturing company that institutes job sharing is included in addition to details on how United Airlines initiated job sharing to avoid layoffs. Meier examines professionals and supervisors as job sharers, changes in family life that are occurring because of job sharing, and how management problems may be resolved via job sharing.

222.   _____. "What Is Happening to Flexitime, Flexitour, Gliding Time, the Variable Day? And Permanent Part-Time Employment? And the Four-Day Week?: The Changing Workplace." *Across the Board* 17 (April 1980): 6-21.

Nollen explains various alternative work phenomena, including why job sharing has become important to individuals preferring permanent part-time employment.

223.   O'Hara, Bruce. *Put Work in Its Place: How to Redesign Your Job to Fit Your Life: The Complete Guide to the Flexible Work Place.* Victoria, B.C.: Work Well Publications, 1988. 258p.

O'Hara includes job sharing as one of the options he recommends for people who want to achieve a balance between work and personal life. Before making a change, one must look at her/his personal needs—money, time, career advancement and satisfaction, as well as work habits. Bibliography.

224. Olmsted, Barney. "Alternative Work Time: A New Tool for Managing." *American Banker* (New York), 5 October 1981, 22+34+40.

According to Olmsted, the interest in alternative work time is due to "changing demographics, value systems, and lifestyles." Job sharing will help organizations meet the flexibility in work schedules that employees are seeking.

225. _____. "Changing Times: The Use of Reduced Work Time Options in the United States." *International Labour Review* 122 (July-August 1983): 479-492.

Job sharing is being utilized by employees wishing to work part-time in positions that in the past have been available only on a full-time basis. Sharers cooperate with each other and work as a team; they are not in competition with one another. Olmsted outlines how two major airlines established job-sharing programs in order to minimize layoffs. Bibliography.

226. _____. "(Flex) Time is Money." *Management Review* 76 (November 1987): 47-51.

Various work time options including job sharing represent major changes from the traditional employment practices and policies. Organizations are seeing employees who are willing to forego salary increases for more time away from the job.

227. _____. "Job Sharing—A New Way to Work." *Personnel Journal* 56 (February 1977): 78-81.

Olmsted defines job sharing, describes its advantages and disadvantages as perceived by both supervisors and workers, and lists ways an employer can introduce the idea of job sharing to an organization.

228. _____. "Job Sharing: A New Way to Work." *Women's Agenda* 1 (May 1976): 3-4.

A description of the effort to develop job-sharing programs by New Ways to Work, a nonprofit vocational resource center that began in 1972 in Palo Alto, California, is the subject of this article. Olmsted, one of the organization's founders, describes their clients and programs in addition to answering several questions employers often ask.

229. _____. "Job Sharing: An Emerging Work Style." *International Labour Review* 118 (May/June 1979): 283-297.

Included in this article are procedures for restructuring a full-time job into one shared by two people. This includes the division of time, tasks, fringe benefits, earnings, and an example of a daily work schedule for each sharer, in addition to a listing of the benefits job sharing can bring to an organization. Bibliography.

230. _____. "When Working Less Means More." *Christian Science Monitor*, 4 January 1979, 23.

Both employees and employers can benefit from part-time employment and job sharing is one of the ways.

231. Olmsted, Barney, and Marcia Markels. *Working Less but Enjoying It More: A Guide to Splitting or Sharing Your Job.* Palo Alto, CA: New Ways to Work, 1978. 77p.

This guide contains short chapters to help those considering job sharing as a means of obtaining a career-oriented part-time position. Steps are given for redesigning a job and approaching an employer. The appendix includes a sample proposal, how to deal with fringe benefits, and examples of where job sharing has been accepted in government positions at the city, county, and state levels. Bibliography.

232. Olmsted, Barney, and Suzanne Smith. *Creating a Flexible Workplace: How to Select and Manage Alternative Work Options.* New York: American Management Association, 1989. 461p.

A comprehensive resource on flexible work arrangements, this book contains descriptions of eight types of work-time alternatives, including flextime, compressed workweeks, regular part-time employment, job sharing, phased/partial retirement, voluntary reduced work-time programs, leave time, and work sharing. The fifty-page chapter on job sharing details the origins of job sharing, its pros and cons, who is using it, when it is appropriate, cost implications, sample schedules, potential problems, and attitudes of all those involved. Bibliography.

233. _____. *The Job Sharing Handbook.* Berkeley, CA: Ten Speed Press, 1985. 199p.

This book is a reprint of *The Job Sharing Handbook* published in 1983 by Penguin Books. (See item No. 234 below.)

234. _____. *The Job Sharing Handbook.* New York: Penguin Books, 1983. 199p.

This handbook was written for the traditional employee interested in job sharing. Chapter headings include: personal and professional assessment, creating a team, presenting the idea to the employer, the first three months, and the future. The text contains numerous (sixteen) illustrations of people who successfully share jobs. Included in the appendix are listings of organizations promoting job sharing and states utilizing job sharing. Bibliography.

235. Olmsted, Daniel. "Visitor from U.K. Shares Information, Inspiration." *Work Times* 4 (Winter 1986): 4+2.

A member of the London-based New Ways to Work, Pamela Walton, visits the San Francisco-based New Ways to Work organization. During her visit, one of the topics is job sharing and how it is working in both countries.

236. "Opportunity for a Government Lead." *IR Digest* (London) 10 (November 1982): 15+20.

This article is a review of Sir Philip Goodhart's publication-- *Stand on Your Own Four Feet: A Study of Work Sharing and Job Splitting* (see item No. 79). Goodhart encourages the British government to foster the creation of job-sharing programs.

237. Owen-Cooper, Teresa. "Job Sharing Slowly Gaining in Appeal." *Denver Post*, 1 October 1990, C1+C5.

Two women clerks for the 4th Judicial District Court in Colorado's El Paso County share one position by working alternate two-week periods. One woman received a promotion when she began to job share because the shared position was higher in the personnel classification system than the one she previously held.

238. "P.A. Group Explores Job Sharing." *San Jose* (CA) *Mercury*, 21 May 1975, North/West [Section] 4.

The city of Palo Alto, California, allows employees to choose the option of job sharing but proponents (a group called New Ways to Work) believe it should not be forced on workers.

239. "Pairing, Sharing, and Splitting—Bringing on the Permanent Part-Timer." In *The Future of the Workplace*, by Paul Dickson. New York: Weybright and Talley, 1975, pp. 243-256.

This chapter details the activities of Catalyst, a nonprofit organization founded in 1962 under the direction of Felice Schwartz, in sponsoring changes in the traditional work patterns for women. Catalyst's programs support the permanent part-timer and encourage employers to hire job sharers and paired workers. In the mid-1960s, Catalyst began working with the Massachusetts Department of Public Welfare to hire half-time case workers. It also worked to establish partnership teaching programs in several Massachusetts communities.

240. "Part-Time Work." In *How to Survive Unemployment: Creative Alternatives*, by Robert Nathan and Michel Syrett. London: Institute of Personnel Management, 1981, pp. 94-104.

These pages on part-time employment include a list of several types of jobs (social workers, clerk-typists, librarians, hospital workers, and lawyers, etc.) that are being shared in Britain. Also included is a list of places where prospective part-timers should look for work.

241. "Part-Time Working and Job Sharing." In *Changes in Working Time: An International Review*, by Paul Blyton. London: Croom Helm, 1985, pp. 101-123.

This chapter gives information on job sharing in Britain and includes reasons for its slow growth from both the employer and employee perspectives. Also mentioned is the job-splitting scheme introduced in 1983 by the British government.

242. Paul, Carolyn E. *A Human Resource Management Perspective on Work Alternatives for Older Workers*. Washington, DC: National Commission for Employment Policy, 1983. 22p. ERIC, ED 234 228.

This study includes information on how job sharing can accommodate older employees wishing to phase into retirement. The flexibility job sharing provides can be advantageous to workers (who get a reduced work schedule) and managers (who get an experienced employee while training a new one).

243. _____. *Work Alternatives: A Human Resource Planning Tool for Managing Older Workers.* Washington, DC: National Commission for Employment Policy, 1983. 23p.

This is a reprint (with an added section entitled "Implications for Public Policy") of an earlier study entitled *A Human Resource Management Perspective on Work Alternatives for Older Workers* (see item No. 242 above).

244. Pechman, Susan. "Why Not Negotiate a Shared Job?" *Woman's Day* 44 (28 April 1981): 34+36+118.

Three job-sharing teams describe how and why they proposed and were granted permission to share their work duties. Positions included a job trainer in Portland, Oregon, a secretary in Salt Lake City, Utah, and a speech therapist in Elgin, Illinois.

245. "Permanent Part-Time and Job Sharing." In *Alternative Work Schedules: Integrating Individual and Organizational Needs*, by Allan R. Cohen and Herman Gadon. Reading, MA: Addison-Wesley, 1987, pp. 66-90.

This chapter defines both permanent part-time positions and job sharing in addition to describing how they work. Also included are the advantages and disadvantages to individuals, organizations, and society.

246. "Permanent Part-Time Employment and Job Sharing." In *Alternative Work Patterns: Implications for Worklife Education and Training*, by Jane Shore. Washington, DC: National Institute for Work and Learning, 1980, pp. 23-27. ERIC, ED 200 734.

Job sharing is described in these pages as "a recent off-shoot of permanent part-time employment." It can, however, be more beneficial than traditional part-time work because prorated salaries and benefits are sometimes higher than compensation received by the part-time employee.

247. "Permanent Part-Timers, Job Sharers Receive Benefits." *Employee Benefit Plan Review* (April 1979): 30+90.

Companies are using alternative work schedules such as permanent part-time and job sharing. This article reports that most part-time employees receive some form of benefits.

248. Phillips, Angela. "Job Sharing—Less Cash but a Richer Life?" *Cosmopolitan* (British ed.) (October 1982): 115+117+120-121.

Married women employees often find too many duties can cause stress and strain both at home and at work. According to Phillips, the Swedish government allows parents a more flexible leave schedule than does the British government. She argues for the reorganizing of work schedules to meet the interests and needs of women workers who also have child-rearing responsibilities.

249. _____. "Jobs: To Split or to Share?" *Cosmopolitan* (British ed.) (April 1983): 45.

Phillips explains why women who could benefit from job sharing will not benefit from job splitting. Split jobs are available only to workers facing unemployment and guidelines set a minimum of fifteen hours per week for each person to work. Job sharing would allow women who have left the workforce to return and sharers who work sixteen hours or more per week would be entitled to benefits.

250. _____. "A Share of the Action." *Observer* (England), 3 July 1988, 37.

In an unprecedented movement, two women share the presidency of the London-based National Union of Journalists. They decided to run for the office on a job-sharing ticket because they had previously shared an executive position, agreed on the issues, and wanted to prove that job sharing works.

251. Pilate, Cheryl. "Job Sharing: A Boon to All Parties." *Wichita* (KS) *Eagle*, 2 June 1980, B5.

Job-sharing pioneers Suzanne Smith and Barney Olmsted, who work for the California-based New Ways to Work firm, visit Wichita and speak to the Chamber of Commerce about the advantages of job sharing.

252. Polsky, Walter L., and Loretta D. Foxman. "Can Job Sharing Work for You?" *Personnel Journal* 66 (September 1987): 30+32-33.
    This article lists reasons why greater productivity can be achieved through job sharing. It also includes questions for prospective job sharers and organizations that are considering instituting job-sharing programs. Sources are given for additional information on alternative work-time options.

253. Porter, Sylvia. "Flexibility in Work Time." *San Francisco Chronicle*, 4 June 1976, 62.
    Job sharing is one way of allowing employees flexibility in their work schedules.

254. _____. "Flexible Work Schedules Undergoing Test Programs." *Star-Bulletin and Advertiser* (Honolulu), 13 June 1976, B4.
    Job sharing can create work alternatives for older employees, students, and working mothers. Porter reports that New Ways to Work in Palo Alto, California, is developing job-sharing programs and sponsoring workshops to explain the idea to both employers and workers.

255. Power, Mike. "Job Sharing Co-Directors Join NWW Board." *Work Times* 5 (June 1987): 5.
    This article announces that two women (who also happen to be job sharers) are joining the Board of Directors of New Ways to Work located in San Francisco. These women share the directorship of the Women's Economic Agenda Project (WEAP) in Oakland, California.

256. Quinn, Jane Bryant. "Opportunities Improving for People Who Want to Work Part-time." *Washington Post*, 27 May 1985, WB35.
    More companies are allowing part-time employment in order to save money and meet the needs of their employees. Pilot job-sharing programs are appearing among teachers and state employees. Most job sharers, however, come from workers already employed by the system.

257. Ramirez, Sylvia. "When Half a Job Is Better Than One." *San Francisco Business* (September 1981): 26-28.

    Guided by employment counselors at New Ways to Work in San Francisco, various individuals (retirees, mothers returning to work, men who had been laid-off, and others who prefer part-time) have found job sharing to be the employment answer for them. Ramirez describes several situations in the San Francisco area where job sharing is preferred.

258. Rathkey, Paul. "British Trade Unions: An Overview." *Work Times* 2 (July 1984): 1+3-4.

    Rathkey discusses the trade union's viewpoint on several new flexible work arrangements that are being used in Britain. These include part-time work, compressed workweeks, shift work, and job sharing.

259. Rawlings, Katherine, and Marian F. Ward. "Two-Timing the Time Clock." *Dynamic Years* 20 (July-August 1985): 54-57.

    These authors believe job sharing is for people in transition--working mothers and those who are changing careers, easing into retirement, wanting a lighter work load, or wishing to continue their education. Included are six steps for sharing and information on three couples who successfully share their jobs.

260. "Reappraisal of Job Sharing Shows Variety of Motives." *Personnel Management* 15 (June 1983): 17.

    This article summarizes various workers' and managers' opinions of job sharing.

261. Reihman, Jacqueline, and Susan J. Bennett. *New Ways to Work / Survey.* Madison, WI: University of Wisconsin-Extension, Institute of Governmental Affairs, 1977. 33p.

    This booklet reports on a survey of Madison, Wisconsin, city employees concerning their opinions of alternative work patterns--including job sharing. Approximately 500 employees returned their questionnaires. A copy of the survey instrument is included as well as results broken down by departments. Employees indicated a strong interest in flexible work schedules. Bibliography.

262. Ricci, Claudia. "Sell Job Sharing to Your Boss." *Working Mother* (November 1988): 38+40+42.

     Ricci discusses finding the right partner and the right job in addition to writing a job-sharing proposal (including information on work schedules, communication, how to overcome disadvantages, costs to the company, and pointers on meeting with the boss).

263. Rich, Les. "Job Sharing: Another Way to Work." *Worklife* 3 (May 1978): 2-6.

     This article contains several examples of workers across the United States who are sharing their jobs with others.

264. Roberts, Alison A. "Splitting the Load." *Sacramento Union*, 17 February 1985, E1+E6.

     Various people in professional positions are taking advantage of job-sharing opportunities because they want freedom from their jobs to do other things. While most women and men want time to spend with their families, others pursue hobbies or different career opportunities.

265. Rogin, Sandra. "Public Sector Pioneers Work Time Alternatives." *Work Times* 5 (Winter 1987): 1+4+8.

     Rogin reports on a survey of personnel officers at the state level concerning the use of alternative work-time options. A chart details individual states reporting the various options (flextime, compressed workweek, permanent part-time, job sharing, voluntary reduced work time, phased retirement, and work sharing).

266. Rosley, Joan. "Job Sharing Offers Innovative Opportunities." *Tempe (AZ) Daily News*, 28 January 1982, B6.

     Dual-career couples can benefit from job sharing because it allows one person the flexibility of a career and time at home. Employers praise part-time employees for their high-productivity levels.

267. Rossi, Paulette. "Flexible Ways to Work: A Viable Nine-to-Five Alternative." *Portland Magazine* 8 (December 1981): 24-25.

Established in Portland, Oregon, in July 1978, Flexible Ways to Work promotes the use of part-time employees. The group operates a job bank for the benefit of both men and women who prefer an alternative to the full-time work schedule. They also promote the idea that part-time employment should not be work that is demeaning, down-grading, or on the low end of the pay scale.

268.   Russell, Thyra K. "Alternative Staffing in Libraries: An Annotated Bibliography." *Illinois Libraries* 68 (September 1986): 435-439.

This seventy-six item bibliography contains citations and annotations for books and periodicals on alternative staffing (flextime, permanent part-time, job sharing, four-day workweek, dual appointments, staff rotation, and "free-lance" librarianship) in libraries. Each of the job-sharing entries is annotated separately in this present volume.

269.   Sandrin, Nancy. "Calling All Moms! Where the Flexible Jobs Are." *Chatelaine* 64 (November 1991): 90-91+93+95+140-141.

Women account for 45 percent of the Canadian labor force and many desire a balance between work and family commitments. This article details ten major employers of women and lists the flexible work alternatives each company offers. All said job sharing was a viable option.

270.   Saseen, Sandra M. "Part-Time Work and Job Sharing: Here to Stay." *GAO Review* 19 (March 1984): 11-13+38.

This researcher discusses the impact of new work schedules (flextime, permanent part-time, job sharing, compressed workweeks, and work sharing) on the labor force of the 1980s. Included are descriptions of the GAOs part-time policy and other organizations using permanent part-time plans as well as advantages and disadvantages to organizations in general. Bibliography.

271.   Sawyer, Kathy. "The Changing Idea of Work in America." *Capital Times* (Madison, WI), 3 January 1978, 27.

Sawyer points out that flexible work scheduling "is not just a women's issue." Younger and elderly workers in addition to those physically unable to work full-time are joining the ranks of employees switching to job sharing. Six percent of 82,000 full-time Wisconsin state employees indicated an interest in reducing their work schedules.

272. _____. "Job Sharing: Growing Trend." *Washington Post*, 26 December 1977, A1+A11.

Sawyer looks at one way American workers are decreasing time spent on the job. This article gives examples of people who are job sharing and describes both advantages and disadvantages from employer and employee perspectives.

273. _____. "More U.S. Workers Favor Flexible Hours over Pay." *Winnipeg* (Canada) *Free Press*, 4 January 1978, 39.

Flexible work schedules and job sharing are ways in which companies can meet the needs of workers who are more interested in time off than in making more money.

274. "Scheduling for Effectiveness." In *The Employee, Contemporary Viewpoints*, edited by Marie S. Ensign and Laurie Nogg Adler. Santa Barbara, CA: ABC-Clio Information Services, 1985, pp. 25-29.

This chapter contains complete citations and abstracts for six articles on job sharing.

275. Schorer, Jane. "Why Are These Women Smiling?" *Des Moines* (IA) *Register*, 20 August 1982, A15.

Women sharers enjoy their time off because it allows them the freedom needed to meet children and family demands without feeling guilty about interruptions to a daily work schedule.

276. Schroeder, Elgin. "West Germans Jump on the Job-Sharing Bandwagon." *Financial Times* (London), 15 July 1981, 15.

Three secretaries in West Germany share what used to be one full-time and one part-time job. Employers see an advantage because someone is always available to work.

277. Schwartz, Felice N. "New Work Patterns--For Better Use of Womanpower." *Management Review* 63 (May 1974): 5-12.

Schwartz promotes several forms of part-time employment (including paired/shared positions) that will meet the needs and abilities of college-educated women who wish part-time work responsibilities.

278. Scordato, Christine, and Julie Harris. "Workplace Flexibility." *HR Magazine* 35 (January 1990): 75-78.

Researchers from Catalyst (an organization working to expand women's career opportunities) report on their study of fifty companies and personal interviews with employees (and their managers) at seventeen companies that offer some type of flexible work environment. One finding indicated that part-time employment and job sharing allow for the retaining of women after they take maternity leaves. Supervisors see the advantage of keeping good employees in whom they have invested a great deal of time and training.

279. Scragg, Dana. "Job Sharing." *AUSTIN Magazine* (Chamber of Commerce, Austin, TX) 24 (July 1982): 47-52.

The Austin, Texas, Women's Center, an organization promoting job sharing, practices what it preaches. Administrators of the center are job sharers who work with the Women's Employment Advocacy to encourage employers to offer options to the forty-hour workweek. Scragg describes several job-sharing positions in Austin and elsewhere in addition to explaining how the job-sharing option benefits both employees and employers. Problem areas are also pointed out.

280. Sedley, Ann, and Lil Stevens. "Job Sharing?" *Morning Star* (London), 15 May 1984, 4.

The authors see job sharing as an opportunity and positive step for women who want something other than the traditional full-time workweek. They say job sharing should not be confused with the British government's job-splitting scheme, which they view as a scheme to withhold women's statutory rights from them.

281. Sermersheim, Kristy. "Profile: Job Sharing Position Sets a Precedent." *Work Times* 5 (Spring 1987): 3.

The author describes her efforts at establishing a shared position for the San Jose, California, office of the Service Employees International Union. Not wishing to lose two good, experienced business agents, she helped establish (over doubts from her executive board) a shared-time plan that works.

282. Shanks, Katherine. "Working Less and Enjoying It More: Alternative Work Schedules." *Wilson Library Bulletin* 59 (October 1984): 106-108+158.

    Job sharing allows for an increase in the quantity and quality of part-time positions. This alternative work schedule promotes the coordination of career and family responsibilities while at the same time benefiting the organization.

283. "Sharing Jobs." In *Part-Timers, Temps, and Job Sharers*. London: Income Data Services, 1985, pp. 86-90.

    Included in this chapter is a general discussion of job splitting and job sharing as well as the joint employment of a married couple.

284. "Sharing Jobs Shows Appeal." *Industrial Society Magazine: IS* (June 1987): 4.

    This article describes job sharing in general, indicating it is more widely available in the public sector than in the private sector. However, private companies and the British government are beginning to support the job-sharing movement. London's New Ways to Work receives almost daily requests for information on flexible work arrangements.

285. Shaw, Ann. "They're Caring and Sharing to Meet the Changing Face of Work." *Glasgow* (Scotland) *Herald*, 10 November 1982, 10.

    Changes in employment behavior have provided employers with evidence that more and more groups of workers are willing to trade income for time spent off the job. One way for management to react to this change is to adopt flexible work arrangements. This article contains a sketch of two women who job share in Edinburgh. Neither sees any disadvantages to the program.

286. Sheehan, Hal. "Over Mechanicville Way." *Schenectady* (NY) *Gazette*, 13 December 1980, 5.

In his column, the author comments on the job-sharing activities of two women who write news releases and produce publications for a medical center in New York City.

287. Smith, Hal. "Confessions of a Job Sharer." *Training* (Minneapolis, MN) 26 (July 1989): 70.

Although many employers may view job sharing as a "perk," the author feels that workers who want to break away from the traditional work pattern should convince their supervisors that it will work.

288. Smith, Jerald R. "Alternative Work Patterns: Job Sharing." *Manage* 33 (April 1981): 31-32.

The author describes job sharing as an alternative to full-time work that allows a "better balance of work and other activities" for many individuals. Costs and benefits to the organization are given as well as a review of the job-sharing survey sponsored by the W.E. Upjohn Institute for Employment Research in 1978 and conducted by Gretl Meier. (See item No. 204 for more information.) Bibliography.

289. Sommer, Kim L., and Deborah Y. Malins. "Flexible Work Solutions." *Small Business Reports* 16 (August 1991): 29-32+34-40.

Sommer and Malins are administrators at an employment and counseling firm responsible for providing middle and executive managers with flexible work solutions. They explain ways in which job sharing meets the definition of "flexible" work. Included are other methods (part-time, flextime, and telecommuting) of meeting the demands of employers.

290. Spittles, David. "Doing It by Halves." *Ideal Home* 122 (June 1981): 142-143.

In addition to reviewing job sharing in Britain, the author details where it is taking place. He then describes the work done by Adrienne Boyle with the London-based "Job Sharing Project" that began in 1977.

291. Stackel, Leslie. "The Flexible Work Place." *Employment Relations Today* 14 (Summer 1987): 189-197.

Job sharing is one form of employment opportunity offered workers wanting part-time work. Benefits derived by the Rolscreen Company in Pella, Iowa, after its initiation of a 1975 job-sharing program are identified.

292. Stark, Gail. "Challenging the Traditional Work Week." *Bellingham (WA) Herald*, 8 October 1989, C1+C3.

Stark talks with Barney Olmsted of New Ways to Work in San Francisco about why more companies are incorporating job sharing into their personnel policies. Olmsted says job sharing can help alleviate concerns about retaining good employees, continuity on the job, and scheduling during peak periods and vacations.

293. Stockard, Jean, and Joan Kalvelage. *A Selected Annotated Bibliography on Job Sharing.* Eugene, OR: Center for Educational Policy and Management, University of Oregon, 1977. 10p. ERIC, ED 139 125.

This bibliography contains twenty-nine entries dealing primarily with part-time employment. The few items covering job sharing are included in the present work.

294. Syrett, Michel. *Employing Job Sharers, Part-Time and Temporary Staff.* London: Institute of Personnel Management, 1983. 118p.

Syrett devotes a third of this book to job sharing. He describes recent developments, job sharing in theory and in practice, and implementation programs in addition to case studies of four different organizations--GEC Telecommunications, London Stock Exchange, Fox's Biscuits, and the Sheffield City Council. Included in the appendix are several examples of job-sharing policies. Bibliography.

295. _____. "Full-Time Perks in Part-Time Work." *Times* (London), 28 June 1987, 83.

According to the author, job sharing in Britain is on the rise. Many local governments offer job-sharing contracts and private organizations are beginning to do the same.

296. _____. "How to Make Job Sharing Work." *Personnel Management* 14 (October 1982): 44-47.

This article examines the advantages and disadvantages of job sharing. Potential problems are pointed out and solutions are given. Bibliography.

297. _____. "Job Sharing Is a Credible Option." *Times* (London), 5 August 1982, 19.

In an effort to fight unemployment, the British government has offered grants to employers who offer job splitting. This plan has received mixed reviews.

298. _____. "Sharing Out the Assets." *Times* (London), 4 February 1982, 23.

The advantages of job sharing have helped to make it an effective alternative to the traditional forty-hour workweek. Reasons for this are cited as well as examples of where job sharing is taking place.

299. Taylor, Linda. "Job Sharing—Can It Work?" *Benefits Canada* 6 (September/October 1982): 8+10.

Hiring officials are not happy about part-time positions when it means extra work and increased costs for them even though the demand for flexible work schedules seems to be on the rise. On the other hand, employers are accepting job sharing more readily than they did in the 1970s because workers have proven its success.

300. Taylor, Marianne. "Job Sharing: Splitting the Workload Can Be Surprisingly Simple." *Chicago Tribune*, 12 April 1981, Section 12, 1+4.

Taylor reports on the working relationship of job-sharing teams at Hewitt Associates in Lincolnshire, Illinois, and Walgreen's in Deerfield, Illinois. Questions and concerns from the employers' points of view are also given.

301. Thrall, Jane. "Sharing Jobs in a 9-to-5 World: When 1 Plus 1 Equals 1." *San Francisco Examiner*, 18 December 1985, C5.

Thrall discusses work-time options with Linda Marks, client program coordinator at San Francisco's New Ways to Work, an organization that provides workshops for people interested in alternatives to the traditional workweek. Examples include women who find job sharing an ideal way to continue their careers while maintaining family commitments.

302. "Three-Fourths of Job Sharers Are Women, Stanford Study Finds." *Education and Work* 5 (23 January 1979): 6-7.

This article reports on the findings of researcher Gretl Meier who surveyed 238 job sharers in 135 jobs in the United States. The complete study is cited in item No. 204.

303. "Time Sharing." In *Developing Women's Management Programs: A Guide to Professional Job Reentry for Women*, by Judie Zubin. Newton, MA: Women's Educational Equity Act Publishing Center, 1982, pp. 95-99. ERIC, ED 217 805.

Time sharing as described in this chapter has the same meaning as job sharing. The concept was adopted by women interns participating in the Women's Management Development Project initiated at Goucher College in 1977. The project was designed to meet the professional career aspirations of women re-entering the labor force.

304. "Toward Career Part-Time Employment: Job Sharing and Work Sharing." In *Permanent Part-Time Employment: The Manager's Perspective*, by Stanley D. Nollen, Brenda Broz Eddy, and Virginia Hider Martin. New York: Praeger, 1978, pp. 155-169.

This chapter defines "career part-time" to include those employees who spend their entire career working part-time and those who spend only a portion of a full-time career working part-time. Job sharing is adaptable to both and has been supported by supervisors and workers in addition to some labor unions.

305. Turner, Tessa. "Job Sharing and Equal Opportunities." *Initiatives* 3 (August 1986): 26-28.

Turner reviews job sharing, who is participating, how to get started, the disadvantages, and the attitudes of trade unions. She also lists and describes the activities of several organizations that are promoting this alternative to the traditional work schedule.

306. "Two for the Price of One." *Time* 107 (3 May 1976): 68.

Although future U.S. Senator Gaylord Nelson's 1937 request for job sharing in a cannery was turned down, this employment practice has increased in popularity. *Time* reports on why this is happening and identifies several job-sharing partners.

307. "Two People One Job: An IR-RR Review of Job Sharing." *Industrial Relations Review and Report* (June 1980): 5-9.

Included in this report are the pros and cons of job sharing and the identification of several organizations in the United Kingdom that have implemented job-sharing programs. Procedures are given for physicians who share a hospital post at the Lothian Health Board in Scotland.

308. Vance, Mary A. *Job Sharing: A Bibliography*. Monticello, IL: Vance Bibliographies, 1984. 5p.

This bibliography contains sixty entries (periodicals and books) on the topics of job sharing and work sharing. Each of the job-sharing entries is included in this present work.

309. "Variations on 'the Job' Theme." *Homemaker's: Canada's Authoritative Women's Magazine* 18 (September 1983): 68.

Job sharing is defined, described, and identified as an alternative to full-time employment.

310. "Varying Hours--Part-Time Work, Job Sharing and Overtime." In *Time Innovations and the Deployment of Manpower: Attitudes and Options*, by Paul Rathkey. Aldershot, Hants., England; Brookfield, VT: Avebury, 1990, pp. 73-97.

This chapter defines job sharing, describes its development in addition to its applications in Britain, and distinguishes the differences between job sharing and job splitting. Bibliography.

311. Verespej, Michael A. "The New Workweek." *Industry Week* 238 (6 November 1989): 11-12+14+16+20-21.

Job sharing is just one of the ways companies are allowing for change in work schedules. Employers feel flexibility is good for their business. It means an employee will be "happy, contented, and more productive." Also featured are profiles of job sharers who prefer the flexible work schedule.

312. Voell, Paula. "Job Sharing: Ideal Solution to Home-Career Dilemma Still Rare." *Buffalo* (NY) *News*, 17 December 1987, D1+D2.

Public information officers at Canisius College in Buffalo, New York, split their job into specific responsibilities. However, they do not receive any benefits because they are part-time employees. The article also describes other employers in the Buffalo area that are offering job sharing to their employees.

313. Wallace, Joan. "Part-Time Work: A New World." *Canadian Home Economics Journal* 36 (Spring 1986): 56-58.

Wallace reviews three types of part-time work--phased retirement, job sharing, and paid leaves. A national survey of Canadian job sharers found that most sharers are women who want to combine a career with family responsibilities. It also revealed that fewer men are job sharing in Canada than in the United States and Great Britain.

314. Walton, Pam. *Job Sharing: A Practical Guide*. London: Kogan Page, 1990. 150p.

Walton presents a useful guidebook, beginning with background information on job sharing, why and what jobs are shared (including specific examples), getting a shared job, making it work, which employers (private, public, and voluntary) hire job sharers, and the trade union's position on job sharing as well as employees' rights and benefits. Several case studies from various types of employment are also included. Bibliography.

315. _____. "Job Sharing." In *New Patterns of Work*, edited by David Clutterbuck. Aldershot: Gower; New York: St. Martin's Press, 1985, pp. 110-126.

In this chapter, Walton reviews job-sharing endeavors in the late 1970s in the United States and the United Kingdom (and in West Germany in the 1980s). She also includes the job-splitting scheme (introduced by the British government in 1983) and tells why it was condemned and by whom.

316. _____. "Updates from Overseas." *Work Times* 5 (Spring 1987): 1+3+7.

    Walton identifies British central and local government authorities that have introduced job-sharing schemes. Most of the negotiating has been handled by two unions--the National and Local Government Officers Association (NALGO) and the National Union of Teachers (NUT).

317. Ward, Debra J. "Job Sharing as an Alternative to Traditional Work Schedules." M.S.S. thesis, Utah State University, 1983. 68p.

    After reviewing the history of job sharing, its issues, and effects, Ward undertook, as part of her thesis, interviews of five job sharers in a hospital accounting department. Job satisfaction and personal fulfillment were rated highly among the sharers. Bibliography.

318. Webb, Trevor. "A Job Shared Can Be an Economic Problem Halved." *Guardian* (London), 3 June 1981, 19.

    The British may see a solution to unemployment and labor productivity problems if job-sharing projects are undertaken.

319. Weinberg, Frances. "Job Sharing in Practice." *Personnel Executive* 1 (August 1981): 32-34.

    Ways in which employers can benefit from job sharing are given in this article in addition to quotes from several job-sharing couples praising their work arrangements.

320. "Why Late Retirement Is Getting a Corporate Blessing." *Business Week* (16 January 1984): 69+72.

    A Levi Strauss employee whose health might have forced her into early retirement shares her managerial position with a younger woman.

321. "Why Split Jobs?" *Industrial Relations Review and Report* (11 January 1983): 2-8.

    The differences between job sharing and job splitting are examined in this report. How both schemes work, their origins, hours, pay, and benefits in addition to who is participating are described. Companies using both are identified.

322. Wilson, Sally. "Job Sharing: A Workable Alternative." *American Baby* 44 (January 1982): 10+13.

   A married couple combines parenting with a reduction in their work time. The mother shares a high school teaching position and works in the morning while the father cares for their son. When the mother comes home at noon, the father goes to his part-time computer programming job.

323. Wiltsher, Anne, and Paul Keers. "Job Sharing: How It Works." *Cosmopolitan* (British ed.) (March 1980): 110+112-113+214.

   In this article, five British couples explain why job sharing works for them. While money and the prospects for promotion are reduced, this is offset by more available time to pursue other interests such as community service, advanced degrees, and time with children.

324. Winfrey, Carey. "Job Sharing—A Working Alternative." *New York Times*, 8 January 1980, B5.

   Job sharers at New York Life Insurance Company work a schedule of one week on, one week off. They split wages and benefits and communicate by weekly notes.

325. Wolman, Jonathan. "The Demise of the 9-to-5 Work Week." *San Francisco Examiner & Chronicle*, 20 August 1978, A12+A13.

   Ways in which the workplace will change by the year 2000 are cited. Part-time positions may increase via job-sharing plans that are being promoted by New Ways to Work, an employment resource center located in the San Francisco area.

326. "Women Start Up Job-Sharing Firm." *Chelmsford* (England) *Weekly News*, 19 March 1987, 13.

   To encourage job sharing in England, two businesswomen set up an employment agency that will provide two people or a team to share the duties of a vacant position. (See item No. 113 for a related article.)

327. Work in America Institute. *New Work Schedules for a Changing Society*. Scarsdale, NY: Work in America Institute, 1981. 128p.

   This book contains various pages detailing part-time employment and job sharing, including several surveys where employees indicated they wanted a reduction in full-time work. Recommendations as to how this can be accomplished are stated.

328. "Working Part-Time." In *The Re-Making of Work: Changing Work Patterns and How to Capitalize on Them*, by David Clutterbuck and Roy Hill. London: Grant McIntyre, 1981, pp. 39-73.

This chapter contains a section entitled "job sharers" in which the authors describe the employee advantages of job sharing as follows: increased flexibility, increased opportunities, and the possibility of increased fringe benefits. Employer advantages include these: increased flexibility, reduced absenteeism/turnover, and increased productivity. Examples of where job sharing is taking place in the United States and United Kingdom are given.

329. Wright, Connie. "More Workers Try Job Sharing." *Nation's Cities Weekly* 2 (17 December 1979): 2.

Wright reports several states are passing laws encouraging the use of part-time employment and job sharing. Why this option has become important to many workers and employers is examined as well as its advantages and disadvantages.

330. Young, W. McEwan. "Innovations in Work Patterns." *Personnel Review* 10 (1981): 23-30.

Job sharing (either horizontal or vertical) is one way in which work patterns have changed since the late 1960s. Early experiments of job sharing were felt to appeal to professional people but as the labor market began to change in the 1970s, job sharing became a practical solution for many employees, especially women.

331. Zalusky, John L. "Alternative Work Schedules: A Labor Perspective." *Journal of the College & University Personnel Association* 28 (Summer 1977): 53-56.

Zalusky says job sharing "involves the elimination of a full-time job opportunity to create two part-time jobs." He believes there are too many workers looking for full-time employment who cannot support families on part-time salaries.

332. Zentner, Carola. "The Best of Both Worlds." *Annabel* (December 1981): 20-21.

    Two nursery school teachers prove that careers and children can go together. Highly trained women (legal, medical, and social workers in addition to librarians) report how job sharing has allowed them to work and have time for their families.

333. Zippo, Mary. "Alternative Work Patterns Sweep Western Europe." *Personnel* 59 (January/February 1982): 34-37.

    A survey of 896 executives in ten European countries revealed that organizations in Sweden and Denmark allow job sharing. Executives report it is used to reduce unemployment, increase the number of university graduates in the workforce, grant more leisure time, and reduce overemployment. Job sharing is not common in Germany, however.

Business

334. *ASPA/CCH Survey*. Chicago: Commerce Clearing House, 1987. 15p.

This survey reports on a random sample of American Society for Personnel Administration members who were questioned on their use of alternative work schedules and non-regular employees. The findings are presented in connection with the Commerce Clearing House Human Resource Management Service. The job-sharing section of the report indicates that very few of the 456 participants used job sharing, job pairing, or job splitting. Factors that influenced the companies' decisions to adopt job sharing are given.

335. Alter, JoAnne. *A Part-Time Career for a Full-Time You*. Boston: Houghton Mifflin, 1982. 394p.

This book contains several pointers on job sharing, including its benefits as a form of part-time employment, how to find a shared job, how to pick a partner, and the interview. Included also is a listing of organizations (with addresses) that help part-timers. Bibliography.

336. *Alternative Work Schedule Directory*. Washington, DC: National Council for Alternative Work Patterns, Inc., 1978. 191p.

Included in this book are listings with addresses and descriptive paragraphs of both private and public businesses that have implemented alternative work schedules, including twenty-eight that have job-sharing programs.

337. *Alternative Work Schedules: Changing Times for a Changing Workforce*. Washington, DC: The Bureau of National Affairs, Inc., 1988. 32p.

Discussion on job sharing includes two surveys--one completed in 1986 by the Administrative Management Society and the other in 1985 for the American Management Association. Also described are the job-sharing experiences at the Kettering, Ohio, Medical Center and Northeast Utilities in Stamford, Connecticut.

338. "The Answer to a Working Mum's Prayers." *Oxford* (England) *Mail*, 26 February 1988, 14.

Co-managers of a mail-order business describe why they enjoy job sharing and the benefits their company receives, including an increase in sales.

339. Arbose, Jules R. "Putting 9 to 5 up on the Shelf." *International Management* 36 (October 1981): 16-20.

A survey of European manufacturing firms indicates that few (10 percent) have tried job sharing but many more (70 percent) have instituted other alternative work patterns--flexible working hours, part-time employment, and phased retirement.

340. Avey, Connie Zarek. "Quantity and Quality of Productivity of Job Sharing Nurses Compared to Full-Time Nurses in a Rural Home Health Nursing Agency." M.S. thesis, University of Wyoming, 1986. 104p.

Avey was able to test whether there was a difference between the quantity and quality of productivity between full-time and job-sharing nurses through the use of their scores on audit chart review schedules. The sample consisted of nurses on the Home Health Services Team of the Casper-Natrona County Health Department in Wyoming. Conclusions are that the job-sharing nurse is "more productive quantitatively and equally as productive qualitatively." Included is a copy of the Wyoming Public Health Nursing Audit Chart Review Schedule. Bibliography.

341. Azzarone, Stephanie. "Shorter Hours, Fuller Lives." *Money* 11 (August 1982): 72-74+76+78.

The sharing of the assistant city attorney position in Palo Alto, California, is viewed as desirable by two women attorneys, both of whom wanted a part-time professional position.

342. Bahls, Jane Easter. "Getting Full-Time Work from Part-Time Employees." *Management Review* 79 (February 1990): 50-52.

Professionals and consultants in the business world detail the advantages of job sharing and encourage its use. One example is that of a publications editor at the University of Montana who shares her job with another woman.

343. _____. "Two for One: A Working Idea." *Nation's Business* 77 (June 1989): 28-30.

Job sharing can lead to a drop in absenteeism, particularly time off for personal errands. Employers may see a drop in their overtime and recruitment expenses. Some jobs may be easier to divide than others and companies must realize that hiring two people does not mean they can accomplish twice the amount of work. The article includes a sidebar describing two sets of job sharers--sisters who share a bookkeeping job in San Francisco, California, and friends who share a management position in Grand Rapids, Michigan.

344. Baildam, E. M., C. I. Ewing, R. Jones, and M. Cummins. "Job Sharing." *Archives of Disease in Childhood* 66 (March 1991): 282-283.

British pediatricians report that job sharing allows for flexibility in scheduling, managing patients, and helping to reduce stress. The doctors say job sharing is successful if there is "mutual trust, loyalty, flexibility, and a commitment to each other as well as to excellent patient care." Bibliography.

345. Bandy, William D., and W. Gordon Eiland. "Job Sharing in Physical Therapy." *Clinical Management* 4 (January 1984): 28-30.

Two physical therapists describe their sharing of one position in three clinical settings. Advantages, problems, and solutions are given.

346. Bardi, Carol A. "Job-Sharing Alternative Draws Nurses Back to the Hospital." *Hospitals* 55 (16 June 1981): 71-72.

The nursing shortage may be alleviated by the initiation of job-sharing practices that provide a flexible working arrangement for qualified nurses.

347. Belden, Constance Ann Hoveland. "Job Sharing: A Tool for Recruitment and Retention in the Face of Labor Shortages." M.A. thesis, Saint Mary's College of Minnesota, 1990. 52p.

This researcher found that job sharing was being offered at a higher rate in businesses in the Minnesota cities of Rochester, Minneapolis, and Winona than was being reported by most studies in the literature. The majority of the companies in Belden's survey reported success in their experiments with job sharing. She found that companies with a large number of employees (over 500) were most likely to offer job sharing–usually initiated by employers. Most of the sharers, however, were in positions at the low end of the pay scale with limited career growth. Belden concludes her thesis with several recommendations to management to help meet the needs of their organization as well as the changing workforce. Bibliography.

348. Benson, John. "Trade Union Attitudes to Job Sharing in Australia and Some Lessons for the UK." *Industrial Relations Journal* 13 (Autumn 1982): 13-19.

Australian trade unions were questioned about their interest in job sharing, the viability of job sharing in Australia, and its advantages and disadvantages. The results showed minimal union interest, potential problems, and implications for the future. Bibliography.

349. Betancourt, E. Kate M., and Jill D. Lombardi. "Job Sharing in Nursing Management: It Can Work." *Nursing Management* 21 (January 1990): 47-49.

Head nurses describe their job-sharing management position in the postpartum unit at the New Britain General Hospital in Connecticut. Included is an outline showing how their duties and responsibilities (both unit-based and hospital-wide) are divided.

350. Bickerstaffe, George. "Sharing a Job to Spread Employment." *International Management* 36 (November 1981): 47-48.

GEC Telecommunications, a subsidiary of General Electric in the United Kingdom, provides job-sharing opportunities for unemployed young people. The job sharers spend one day a week at college, and after a contract period of eighteen months, GEC usually offers them full-time permanent employment.

351. Bland, Julia. "A Fair Share of Doctoring." *BMA News Review* (British Medical Association) 13 (December 1987): 23.

Job sharers often end up working more than half-time, which is one advantage employers find useful. Women physicians sharing an obstetric position began by dividing the week in half--each working two and a half days. They soon found that half days were inefficient and changed their schedule to two days one week and three days the next week. The British Medical Association maintains a job-share register for those interested in job sharing.

352. Blitzer, Carol G. "Job Sharers Split Benefit Costs at Air Cal." *Business Insurance* 17 (24 January 1983): 20.

Guidelines, including benefits, are spelled out for job sharers at Air California, a regional airline located in Newport Beach, California.

353. Blumenthal, Marcia. "At a Growing Number of Companies, Part-Time Jobs and Job Sharing Offering DP Career Options." *Computerworld* 16 (8 November 1982): 10-11.

Data processing professionals are offered job-sharing positions at Fireman's Fund Insurance Company in San Rafael, California. The company's personnel director describes cost-saving advantages.

354. Bratton, David A. "Moving Away from Nine to Five." *Canadian Business Review* 13 (Spring 1986): 15-17.

The director of human resources at London Life Insurance Company in Canada explains what a flexible work program including job sharing has meant to his employees and his company.

355. Brown, Barbara Jean. "The Viability of Job Sharing in the Anchorage Banking Industry." M.B.A. project, California State University, Sacramento, 1982. 26p.

Brown's research included a formal interview with personnel officers at eleven banking institutions in Anchorage,

Alaska. She found job sharing was not very common--two institutions indicated they employed one job-sharing team each. The others indicated that they had not been approached about the possibility, but several believed it would become an option in the future. Bibliography.

356. Bruce, Margaret. "Job Sharing in the Public Sector: Planning Officer in a General Hospital." *RIPA Report* (Newsletter of the Royal Institute of Public Administration) 8 (Autumn 1987): 8-9.

Bruce describes how she and her job-sharing partner applied for and administer the position of planning officer at Bedford, England's, General Hospital. Also included are statements from their colleagues about the job-sharing arrangement.

357. Buchan, James. "A Share in the Future." *Nursing Times: NT* 87 (5 June 1991): 32-33.

In this article, Buchan reports on a 1989 survey of job sharing in the United Kingdom's National Health Service. Charts are included listing the number of health authorities that reported job sharing, the rationale for its introduction, and the advantages and disadvantages as viewed by health authorities with and without job-sharing positions.

358. _____. "A Shared Future." *Nursing Times, Nursing Mirror* 83 (28 January 1987): 44-45.

Job sharing is seen by the United Kingdom's National Health Service Management Board as a means of solving problems of recruitment and retention. Bibliography.

359. _____. "A Working Alternative." *Senior Nurse* 7 (August 1987): 27.

Buchan comments that the National Health Service has been slow in promoting the use of job sharing to help alleviate the United Kingdom's nursing shortage. Most job-sharing proposals in the nursing field have been set up by the employees themselves rather than being established by management. Bibliography.

360. "Can Job Sharing Work for You?" *Employee Relations Bulletin* (7 April 1982): 6-8.

Job sharing works well for working mothers, retirees, students, and disabled persons. Personnel at Seafirst Mortgage Corporation in Seattle, Washington, describe how positions are split and the benefits derived by sharers and employers.

361. Carlson, Elliot. "Longer Work Life? A Look at the Future of Retirement." *Modern Maturity* 28 (June-July 1985): 22-24+26-28.

Retirees view job sharing as a way of continuing to work (part-time) without affecting their pension or health benefits.

362. Carver, Carol, and Linda J. Crossman. "Job Sharing: It May Be Right for You." *American Journal of Nursing* 80 (April 1980): 676-678.

Nurses who share a job administering and directing a county-wide day-care program for older adults clearly believe the advantages of job sharing outweigh the disadvantages.

363. "Case Studies: Canadian Organizations and Their Family-Related Programs." *Canadian Business Review* 16 (Autumn 1989): 22-26.

The London Life Insurance Company in Ontario has about sixty employees sharing jobs. Sharers receive prorated benefits; managers who had to be convinced job sharing would work now feel confident with its results.

364. Chamberlin, Patricia A., and Mary D. Jones. "Planning a Shared-Schedule Residency." *Journal of Medical Education* 55 (June 1980): 496-501.

Residents in the Department of Pediatrics of the University of Texas Medical Branch at Galveston describe their shared schedules and the problems they encounter.

365. Clarke, Mary Ann, and Anne Stokes. "Sharing the Load of Law Office Management." *Docket Call* 15 (Winter 1981): 5-8.

Co-office managers of a law firm share duties by working every other week. They are responsible for the finances, office equipment, and personnel. Communication is maintained by writing notes to each other.

366.   Clarkson, Eileen, Irene Day, Gloria Mohr, and Doreen Reid.
        "Bread and Roses: Job Sharing in Management." *Dimensions in
        Health Service* 62 (April 1985): 39-41+43.
             Two Canadian social workers obtain a job-sharing position
        and form their own consulting firm. Nursing supervisors take
        part in a shared project; after the position is evaluated,
        administrators decide to make it permanent. Bibliography.

367.   Clutterbuck, David. "Job Sharing Is Winning Wider Support."
        International Management 37 (October 1982): 44, E6+E8.
             The United Kingdom officially supports job sharing. Seen
        by many as a means of diminishing unemployment, businesses
        such as GEC Telecommunications have become directly
        involved in providing job-sharing opportunities.

368.   Collins, Helen Lippman. "A Full-Time Job for Part-Time
        Nurses." *RN* 52 (June 1989): 18+20.
             Twin nurses share a single job at Rush-Presbyterian-St.
        Luke's Medical Center in Chicago. Tips for finding a suitable
        partner and approaching management about job-sharing
        possibilities are included in this article.

369.   Collins, Joanne A., and Anne-Marie Krause. "Improving
        Productivity through Job Sharing." *Business Forum* 9 (Summer
        1984): 4-7.
             Job sharing is described here as a way for a company to
        maximize the use of its human resources. Relevant questions
        and guidelines are included for the benefit of a company
        considering the implementation of a job-sharing program.

370.   Conrad, Judy. "What's Happening...in Nova Scotia." *Canadian
        Nurse* 77 (September 1981): 47-48.
             The author and another nurse share the position of evening
        administrative supervisor at Roseway Hospital in Shelburne,
        Nova Scotia. Their work schedule is seven days on, seven days
        off.

371.   Coolidge, Joy. "Employer Gets 2 Secretaries for Price of 1."
        Arizona Republic, 17 January 1982, D1+D3.

Legal secretaries describe how they make their job-sharing arrangement work and still achieve the family life they desire.

372. Coste, Chris. "Staying Whole as Halves: Cook County's Part-Time Interns." *New Physician* 26 (February 1977): 35-36.

By working every other month, interns at Chicago's Cook County Hospital balance their education and other interests. They feel the shared experience has been very helpful in making the transition from student to physician.

373. Cregar, Michael. "Flextime Continues to Edge Upward." *Management World* 17 (July/August 1988): 14-15.

Cregar indicates a decrease in the number of companies that have job-sharing plans in place or under consideration.

374. Davis, Lorraine. "Having It All–Legally." *Vogue* 175 (June 1985): 76.

A job-sharing experiment of sixteen months resulted in lawyers in the New York State Department of Law being given permanent opportunities to participate in job sharing.

375. DeFrancis, Carol. "Work Time Alternatives in Health Care: Create Solutions to Modern Needs." *Work Times* 6 (Spring 1988): 1+6.

The author reports on employees in the health care field who are successfully job sharing. These include residents at the Harvard Medical School and pediatric interns at Stanford University in addition to nurses at Ohio's Kettering Medical Center and the State of Hawaii.

376. Dempster, Doug. "One Job, but Two Fill Boss Position." *Sacramento Bee*, 4 October 1977, B1+B3.

A man and a woman share the executive director position of the Lung Association in Sacramento, California. Officially, one is listed as executive director and the other as a consultant. In practice, though, they both work half-time and divide the responsibilities of the job.

377. DePaolis, Mark. "How 2 M.D.s = 1 1/2 Practices = 1 Happy Couple." *Medical Economics* 66 (18 September 1989): 169-172.

Married physicians share a medical practice in Minneapolis. Working three-quarter time, each sees some patients exclusively, but they share treatment of families with children. They feel the benefits of this arrangement exceed the loss of income.

378.   Dickason, John H. "Employee Time Sharing Works." *Association Management* 36 (September 1984): 180.

The work schedule of a secretary at the Illinois State Bar Association in Springfield, Illinois, is divided by two women. The work load, however, is not always divided because some projects cannot be passed back and forth.

379.   Dimmock, Stuart. "Splitting and Sharing Jobs." *Nursing Times* 79 (5 October 1983): 60.

The differences between job sharing and job splitting are identified by the author. For nurses who often work part-time, job sharing may provide opportunities for more interesting and better-paying jobs.

380.   "Does Job Sharing Have Potential in Your Business?" *Profit Building Strategies for Business Owners* 19 (July 1989): 9-10.

The following people are often interested in job sharing: retirees, creative artists (writers, painters, actors), job returnees, and people who are willing to sacrifice salary for a more relaxed work schedule. Various ways for sharers to communicate include these: telephone, tape recordings, daily log, briefing board, meetings, and shared work time.

381.   Downey, Maureen. "Teamwork." *Atlanta Constitution*, 29 January 1990, B1+B4.

Downey reports on two women who share a bank vice-presidency and are responsible for their clients' investment and loan needs. Both women work three days a week--overlapping on Wednesdays. Each receives 60 percent of a full-time salary. They split holidays and vacation time. The women agree that the success of their arrangement is "based on trust in each other's judgments."

382.   Dunn, Elisabeth. "Half the Job--Twice the Life." *Times* (London), 31 May 1981, 36.

Job sharers (a man and a woman) at the London Stock Exchange enjoy their work as well as the free time it affords them away from the job.

383. Feiden, Karyn, and Linda Marks. *Negotiating Time: New Scheduling Options in the Legal Profession*. San Francisco: New Ways to Work, 1986. 79p.

This book covers leaves (personal, maternity, paternity, etc.), working part-time, and job sharing among attorneys and others in the legal profession. The chapter on job sharing includes initiating a shared position, developing a policy, examples of work schedules, cost analysis, union reactions, and sample interview questions. Included also is a list of nonprofit and professional groups interested in facilitating part-time work among lawyers. Bibliography.

384. Fennell, Edward. "Job Sharing–Two into One Will Go." *Graduate Post* (October 1982): 6-7.

The author looks at job sharing as a way for graduate trainees to fill one position and employers to get two experienced managers for the price of one trainee. It is the responsibility of the employee to find a partner and to sell the idea of job sharing to prospective administrators.

385. Fischel-Wolovick, Lisa, Connie Cotter, Ilene Masser, Emily Kelman-Bravo, Ronnie Sue Jaffe, Gary Rosenberg, and Beth Wittenberg. "Alternative Work Scheduling for Professional Social Workers." *Administration in Social Work* 12 (1988): 93-102.

This article describes a pilot project that initiated three types of alternative work schedules–job sharing, compressed workweeks, and flextime–in a teaching hospital. Although the hospital management had some concerns about accountability, productivity, finances, and timing, a job-sharing position was established. After resolving various problems and working together for two years, the committee studying alternative work schedules believes it has been a positive experience. Bibliography.

386.   Fisman, Sandra, and Lynne Ginsburg. "Part-time Residency Training." *Canadian Journal of Psychiatry* 26 (November 1981): 484-486.
        Following guidelines passed by the U.S. Congress concerning shared-schedule positions in medical residency programs, residents in the Department of Psychiatry at Queen's University, Kingston, Ontario, begin a part-time shared-residency program at Kingston Psychiatric Hospital.

387.   Fitzgerald, Mark. "Job Sharing." *Editor & Publisher* 118 (19 October 1985): 11+36-37.
        Husband and wife newspaper employees find job sharing an ideal situation. Papers in Maryland, Minnesota, and Missouri all employ job sharers and managing editors indicate they are pleased with the employees' performance.

388.   "Flexible Work." *Futurist* 20 (September-October 1986): 47.
        This note is based on the 1986 AMS (Administrative Management Society) Flexible Work Survey which indicated that the use of both flextime and job sharing in businesses was increasing. The 1986 survey reported that 17 percent of U.S. businesses were using job sharing. The survey results are also reprinted in part in *Employee Benefit Plan Review* 41 (December 1986): 91-92 and *Business* (Atlanta) 36 (October-November-December 1986): 58-59.

389.   "The Flexijob Revolution." *Management Today* (February 1983): 105.
        British senior managers explore opportunities and problems arising from job sharing and job splitting. Personnel from GEC Telecommunications say they have many young people waiting to job share because "they see it as a lead-in to real work."

390.   "For More and More Workers, an End to the 9-to-5 Day." *U.S. News & World Report* 82 (4 April 1977): 80-81.
        Businesses and industry are allowing employees to alter traditional work routines through the use of flextime, job sharing, compressed workweeks, and permanent part-time. Sidebar describes the job sharing of two elementary school teachers in Des Moines, Iowa.

391. Foster, Catherine. "Companies Find Job Sharing Can Be a Two-Way Benefit." *Christian Science Monitor*, 30 March 1983, 11.

    Increased productivity, reduced turnover, and flexible scheduling are some of the reasons business executives in the banking, airline, and manufacturing industry approve of job sharing. The Rolscreen Company in Pella, Iowa, employs several job-sharing teams and gets cooperation from workers when it occasionally asks each person to put in a forty-hour week.

392. Franco, Melvi, and Jawanna Stubblefield. "Sharing a Summer Job at NWW." *Work Times* 5 (Summer 1987): 5+7-8.

    Two high school teenagers work for the summer sharing an office position at New Ways to Work in San Francisco, California. Both describe their work experiences and their views on job sharing.

393. Friese, Penny, and Elaine Stefura. "Job Sharing, a Solution to the Personal Energy Crisis." *Canadian Nurse* 79 (January 1983): 20-23.

    Two Canadian nurses report on their interviews with other nurses to determine how job sharing works and to describe its advantages and disadvantages from both the employee's and employer's perspective. Bibliography.

394. Gandi, Ader B. "Corporate Perspectives on Job Sharing." M.S. thesis, San Francisco State University, 1985. 59p.

    Gandi surveyed corporate personnel directors in order "to examine corporate perspectives and attitudes towards job sharing as compared to corporate experiences with job sharing." A majority of the respondents did not think their company had a need for job sharing since part-time workers were always available. On the other hand, managers did not view part-timers as career oriented and felt if job sharers were promoted that problems would develop within their organization. The success of job sharing was due in large part to a change in management's perceptions and attitudes. A copy of the researcher's question-naire is included. Bibliography.

395.   Geltner, Sharon. "Two for the Job of One." *Washington Journalism Review* 7 (September 1985): 38-39.
        Geltner reports on various journalists who share newspaper reporting duties. Most managing editors see advantages to having their employees sharing jobs, but others feel sharers cannot provide the continuous coverage desired by the newspaper.

396.   Gill, Penny. "Flextime." *Stores* 63 (December 1981): 21-24+26+30.
        Job sharing is one form of flextime. Differences between work sharing and job sharing and the advantages of job sharing are included in this article along with comments from Walgreen Drug and B. Dalton supervisors who sponsor job-sharing programs.

397.   "Giving Employees Time, Flexibility." *Employee Benefit Plan Review* 44 (May 1990): 16-18.
        Flexible schedules have become a way of supporting employees with family issues. A 1987 study of 1,200 employers surveyed by the Bureau of Labor Statistics revealed that 15.5 percent had job-sharing options. Companies with a small number of employees were more likely to offer a variety of alternative work schedules than companies with a large number of employees.

398.   Goodwin, Judi. "Two Smart Ladies and Three Nuns." *Shellman* (Shell Oil, UK) (July/August 1980): 9-11.
        This article describes how two women jointly manage for Shell Oil in the United Kingdom a self-service gas station called Three Nuns. They work alternate weeks--each working for seven straight days and then off seven days. They also employ young mothers in rotating shifts, which allows them to be at home with their children after school.

399.   Goold, Christine. "How Job Sharing Works for Me." *McCall's* 109 (March 1982): 20+143.
        A real-estate office secretary tells how her job-sharing position evolved; the secretary advertised in the newspaper for a co-worker and coordinated their schedules and responsibilities.

400. _____. "Try Something New—Job Sharing." *Real Estate Today* 17 (June 1984): 15-16.

Goold reports that her job-sharing experiment has continued for two years due in large part to the flexibility of each partner. She spells out six guidelines to help the reader initiate a workable program.

401. Graham, Ellen. "Flexible Formulas." *Wall Street Journal*, 4 June 1990, R34-R35.

Job sharing is one of the ways companies have been able to offer alternative scheduling to their employees. Although job sharing is not always available to supervisors, it has been available for some time to professional and hourly workers.

402. Haberman, Maxine R., and Judy Weisberg. "Two Are Better Than One (Eccles. 4:9)—Successful Job Sharing in a Nursing Home." *Nursing Homes* 34 (March/April 1985): 36-38.

The benefits of teamwork are described here by two social workers at the Hebrew Home of Greater Washington in Rockville, Maryland. The sharers are responsible for the paperwork and patient-care conferences for one floor of the nursing home and feel strongly that the residents, families, institution, and workers all benefit from the shared position. Bibliography.

403. Hager, Philip. "Job Sharing: Alternative to the 40-Hour Week Gains." *Los Angeles Times*, 23 June 1980, Part 1, 3+24.

Anesthesiologists (and sisters) share a hospital position at the Kaiser-Permanente Medical Center in Oakland, California. Due in large part to the efforts of New Ways to Work in San Francisco, the concept of job sharing has been accepted in California and is spreading to several other states as well.

404. _____. "Sisters Hail Job Sharing, Get 'Best of Two Worlds'." *Chicago Sun Times*, 25 June 1980, 20.

Cited above as item No. 403.

405. Harrison, Patrick. "An Evaluation of the Four Worker Job Sharing Model." M.S.W. thesis, University of Manitoba, 1981. 111p.

This thesis evaluates the four-worker job-sharing model that was developed at the Women's Centre of the Health Services Centre, which is a part of a large medical complex in Winnipeg, Canada. An in-depth case study was conducted on social workers employed by the Women's Centre. The four-worker job-sharing model is slightly different from the traditional half-time job-sharing arrangement in that most of the social workers are employed three-quarters of the time with some overlap. This model is designed to combine the advantages of part-time work while easing the strain felt by some part-timers. Harrison reports on the potential advantages and disadvantages to the individuals as well as the organization. He concludes that this job-sharing model has been a success. Bibliography.

406.   Hildick-Smith, Marion, Gillian Collier, and Vanessa Potter. "The Benefits and Snags of Job Sharing." *Practitioner* 231 (8 January 1987): 9-10.

In setting up a job-sharing arrangement, two problems arise immediately--finding someone in the same area who will agree to share and competing with other full-time applicants. Doctors Collier and Potter spent a profitable year sharing a senior house officer position in geriatric medicine and plan to continue sharing in psychiatry and other fields of study. They split weekend call duty--one is on-call on Saturdays and the other on Sundays. They reverse this schedule at various intervals.

407.   Hinderegger, Jeanne Bates. "Job-Sharing Attitudes of Personnel Managers." M.A. thesis, University of Akron, 1983. 91p.

This researcher sampled seventy-three personnel managers from forty different kinds of businesses in the Akron, Ohio, area and questioned them about their attitudes toward job sharing. Responses are analyzed and a copy of the questionnaire is included. Hinderegger found that job sharing was not widespread. However, companies that have used it are strong supporters of it. Bibliography.

408.   Hymowitz, Carol. "As Aetna Adds Flextime, Bosses Learn to Cope." *Wall Street Journal*, 18 June 1990, B1+B4.

For the past four years, two women have shared a job arranging conferences for Aetna managers. One works the first half of the week and the other the last half. They meet for lunch on Wednesdays. While their boss had reservations at first, he now says he would "welcome an entire staff of job sharers."

409. *Industrial Relations and Job Sharing Arrangements.* [Melbourne]: Faculty of Law, Monash University [1983]. 22p.

This monograph contains the transcripts of three papers that were given at a seminar at Australia's Monash University. One deals with alternative work patterns in general and the other two look at job sharing and are entitled as follows: "Experiments and Possibilities in Job-Sharing Arrangements" by W. A. Howard; "Some Contractual Aspects of Job Sharing" by Ronald Clive McCallum. Examples are included as well as discussion on the demand for job sharing, workers compensation, costs, and negative aspects.

410. "Interview." *Work Times* 1 (Spring 1983): 3-5.

Leonard Grice, personnel director of the United Kingdom's GEC Telecommunications, explains through a series of questions and answers his company's job-sharing program for youth who have dropped out of school.

411. "Ireland–Job Sharing at Aer Rianta." *European Industrial Relations Review* (March 1983): 10-12.

The Irish Airports Authority has agreed with the Federated Workers' Union of Ireland to permit workers to engage in job sharing. Terms and conditions are detailed in a copy of the agreement, which is included in the article.

412. "Is Share-a-Job Here to Stay?" *IPM Digest* (Institute of Personnel Management) 209 (December 1982): 8-9.

The head of personnel at the London Stock Exchange, Rhiannon Chapman, points out that job sharing will be a success if it benefits the organization.

413. Jackson, Mark. "GEC Launches Job-Sharing Scheme." *Times Educational Supplement* (London), 15 May 1981, 1.

In the United Kingdom, GEC Telecommunications is working with unemployed school dropouts in a youth opportunities program that will be expanded to offer these workers eighteen months of job sharing.

414.   *Job Sharing: A Negotiator's Guide.* London: Banking Insurance and Finance Union, 1990. 9p.

This booklet describes job sharing in general, reasons employers are interested in hiring job sharers, and the benefits of job sharing to the Banking Insurance and Finance Union. Included is a negotiating checklist that both employers and potential job sharers could follow when establishing a job-sharing position.

415.   "Job Sharing Becoming Popular as a Working Arrangement." *Chicago Tribune*, 18 September 1979, Section 4, 14.

Two personnel representatives at TRW Vidar in Mountain View, California, had babies at about the same time and persuaded the company to allow them to share one position upon their return to work.

416.   *Job Sharing in Health Care.* San Francisco: New Ways to Work, 1984. 45p. ERIC, ED 269 557.

Divided into two basic parts, this handbook deals with issues and questions (initiation, implementation, proposals, cost analysis, and management) of concern to administrators, supervisors, and potential sharers. Case studies are included for a physical therapist, an oncology counselor, public health nurses, and hospital staff nurses. Bibliography.

417.   "Job Sharing in Industry." *Industrial Society* 64 (June 1982): 16+30.

Officials at GEC Telecommunications in the United Kingdom introduced job sharing to reduce the number of unemployed youngsters (school dropouts). This article describes the work schedule, employee benefits, and the overall advantages of job sharing to employers.

418.   "Job Sharing." In *The Changing Workplace: New Directions in Staffing and Scheduling*, Washington, DC: Bureau of National Affairs, 1986, pp. 63-66.

Job-sharing programs at the Rolscreen Company in Pella, Iowa, and the Kettering Medical Center in Kettering, Ohio, are detailed in these pages.

419. "Job Sharing—The Rolscreen Co." In *Work & Family: A Changing Dynamic*. Washington, DC: Bureau of National Affairs, 1986, pp. 78-80.

These pages describe the job-sharing "team program" that began in 1975 at the Rolscreen Company in Pella, Iowa. The program is generally limited to assembly-line jobs where the duties are repetitious. Partners decide between themselves how to divide the work hours and management approves so long as they accomplish the tasks. Bibliography.

420. *Job Sharing through Collective Bargaining*. San Francisco: New Ways to Work, 1982. 19p.

This booklet suggests several items that union officials should review for incorporation into a job-sharing collective bargaining contract. These include the following: defining the bargaining unit, fringe benefits, seniority scheduling, overtime, assuring the program is voluntary, and questions concerning returning to full-time work. Sections from sample contracts are quoted.

421. Jones, Rosamond, and Mary Cummins. "Job Sharing: A Real Option." *Maternal and Child Health* 15 (March 1990): 79-81.

The authors jointly applied for and were granted a shared pediatric post in the Ealing General Hospital in Middlesex, England. They planned the division of duties before they applied for the job. They found that colleagues were often curious about the costs and contracts of the shared position. Bibliography.

422. Kleiman, Carol. "2-for-1 Plan Growing in Popularity with Employers, Employees." *Chicago Tribune*, 19 August 1991, Section 4, 5.

Suzanne Smith and Barney Olmsted, co-founders and co-directors of New Ways to Work in San Francisco, say job-sharing opportunities have been increasing since they started their organization in 1972. Women who have been job sharing together since 1983 have assumed (jointly) the presidency of the First Chicago Highland Park Bank. Since the bank is open six days a week, they each work three days a week with no overlap. They share the salary and benefits.

423. Kricorian, Nancy. "Job Sharing: Potential for Part-Time Workers." *Union W.A.G.E.* (Women's Alliance to Gain Equality) (November-December 1980): 1.

Local unions of the Service Employees International Union in Santa Clara County, California, have negotiated a contract that calls for the sharing of full-time positions.

424. Krier, Beth Ann. "Job Sharing: When One Job Equals Teamwork." *Los Angeles Times*, 30 November 1980, Part 7, 1+16-18.

Both United Airlines and Pan Am have initiated job-sharing programs for flight attendants, thus preventing massive layoffs. Seven nuclear medical technologists at the Cancer Foundation in Santa Barbara, California, also share five jobs because it provides each of them with a more flexible schedule.

425. Kushner, Sherrill. "Job Sharing: A Professional Alternative." *Loyola Reporter* (Los Angeles, CA), 29 September 1982, 5.

Kushner details the type of worker who would desire a shared position and explains why job sharing is becoming a viable alternative for lawyers wishing to reduce their work time. Examples are given of lawyers in the California cities of Palo Alto and San Francisco who enjoy the balance between work and personal time that job sharing affords them.

426. _____. "Job Sharing: An Alternative to a Traditional Law Practice." *Legal Economics* 11 (November/December 1985): 24-28.

Job sharing not only functions as an alternative to employee layoffs but can also allow corporations under a hiring freeze to employ affirmative action candidates or to pair workers of different skills or experience. California attorney positions in Palo Alto and San Francisco are described in this article as well as a husband-and-wife team who share the legal caseload of the Assistant U.S. Attorney's office in Portland, Oregon. Job sharing for lawyers in the State Attorney General's office in New York State has been established on a permanent basis, thus eliminating the need to negotiate on a one-to-one basis.

427. _____. "Job Sharing: The Employer's Perspective." *Loyola Reporter* (Los Angeles, CA), 1 December 1982, 2+4.

In this continuation of a previous article (see item No. 425), the author identifies several reasons why employers readily accept job sharing as an innovative work arrangement. Job sharing can minimize burnout and allow for more creative problem solving in addition to reducing absenteeism and turnover.

428. Kuzins, Rebecca. "Women Attorneys Opt for Part-Time Jobs in Law Firms." *Los Angeles Daily Journal*, 30 March 1984, 1+16.

While some legal work (major litigation) may not lend itself to part-time work, other positions, such as those in tax and estate planning, might. Part-time work does not always mean handling boring routine work on a half-time (usually twenty hours) basis but can mean working forty hours a week instead of seventy or eighty hours, as many lawyers do.

429. Lathlean, Judith. *Job Sharing a Ward Sister's Post.* Peterborough, England: Ashdale Press, 1987. 41p.

Researcher Lathlean examines job sharing in the British Health Service, particularly at Charing Cross Hospital. After reviewing the literature, she describes the job-sharing position she will evaluate, and provides details of the six-month evaluation. Included are the effects job sharing has on hospital staff, patients, and their relatives as well as each of the ward sisters. Bibliography.

430. Lawson, Carol. "With Job Sharing, Time for the Family." *New York Times*, 1 June 1989, C1+C6.

Job-sharing advocates (academicians, public officials, and women's groups) see it as a way of allowing flexible scheduling for working parents. In the beginning, only clerical or technical positions were shared. Now it has been introduced into managerial and professional levels of employment. Corporations have been reluctant to embrace job sharing although it is being accepted by businesses that do not want to lose valuable employees.

431.   Lee, Patricia. "Job Sharing—A Concept Whose Time Has Come." *Office Administration and Automation* 45 (April 1984): 28-30+88.

Office automation may contribute to an increase in job-sharing positions. In this article Lee includes a checklist of ten steps to be followed for successful planning of a job-sharing program.

432.   Leighton, Patricia. "Bridging the Skills Shortage: Job Sharing." *Industrial Society Magazine: IS* (December 1988): 21-23.

Job sharing can be successful in both the public and private sectors. Leighton stresses the need for effective management and suggests "a need for a clear and consistent view of what job sharing means in the individual organization, a commitment to it from all levels, and a willingness to review and adapt personnel and managerial procedures."

433.   Lempp, Heidi, and Angela Heslop. "Pioneering Spirit." *Senior Nurse* 7 (August 1987): 24-26.

Two nurses at London's Charing Cross Hospital share the management of a medical ward. Both had experience running the ward full-time and both wanted to change to part-time work. Job sharing brings up questions of accountability. Can one sharer be held accountable for the other's mistakes? These nurse-managers believe that the position should be viewed as a whole, rather than as individual duties, and that while on duty each person is to be held accountable and responsible. Bibliography.

434.   Levine, James A. "Job Sharing: How One Couple Does It." *Working Woman* 1 (December 1976): 57-59.

Printshop owners share their printing business and child care of their two-year-old son. After convincing their business associates, their parents, and themselves they were doing the right thing, they found many advantages of working together in the shop and at home.

435. Lott, Jeanne. "With a Changing Work Force, Has Job Sharing's Time Arrived?" *San Diego Business Journal* (10 January 1983): 1+8-10.

The schedules of many workers now include flextime, work sharing, and job sharing. This can be attributed to many things, including more women and single parents in the labor force, elderly workers wishing to phase into retirement, and (sometimes) a sluggish economy. In order for job sharing to work, it takes a commitment on both sides--employer and employee. Sidebar includes a list of benefits enjoyed by employers.

436. Lum, Donald C. "Guest Opinion." *Office Administration and Automation* 45 (January 1984): 100.

It is the opinion of this vice-president of personnel at Pfizer, Inc., in New York that job sharing can and does work. His company has employed job-sharing secretaries who cooperate, communicate, and share a sense of responsibility, all of which are necessary for job efficiency.

437. "Managers 'Unconvinced' on the Benefits of Job Sharing." *Personnel Management* 20 (August 1988): 8.

An Institute of Manpower Studies report examined the view of job sharing at thirty companies. Managers felt too many positions, especially supervisory ones, were unsuitable for job sharing. They also predicted an increase in financial costs if job sharing were implemented. They were not convinced that the benefits would outweigh the costs.

438. Marks, Linda. "A New Way to Work: Job Sharing." *Chemtech* 18 (November 1988): 646-648.

This article is adapted from a presentation the author gave at a national meeting of the American Chemical Society. In her description of new trends in chemical employment, the author detailed job sharing as a possibility; in this article she outlines what job sharing is, how it is accomplished, and salary and fringe benefits as well as the advantages to an employer.

439. _____. *Survey on Work Time Options in the Legal Profession: San Francisco and Alameda Counties: Final Report.* San Francisco: New Ways to Work, 1986. 31p.

   Marks surveyed legal organizations in San Francisco and Alameda counties that employed three or more attorneys concerning their use of alternative employment practices (part-time employment, job sharing, flextime, and leaves). Job sharing was reported by seven attorneys and twenty-five non-attorneys in the responding organizations.

440. Marshall, Janice Rademaker. "Job Sharing and Voluntary Reduced Worktime Options: The Union Perspective." Ph.D. diss., University of Oregon, 1982. 295p.

   Researcher Marshall reports on a survey she undertook to determine union attitudes toward job sharing and to analyze ways to gain support for job-sharing programs. Included are case studies of unions which have both supported and opposed job-sharing proposals. Bibliography.

441. Martin, Pamela. "Why Consider Job Sharing?" *Practitioner* 232 (22 November 1988): 1259.

   Martin believes job sharing is useful to doctors because they are able to follow a schedule that meets their needs. She feels that if physicians are not allowed to engage in flexible scheduling, there could be a decrease in the number of practicing doctors.

442. McDowall, Joan. "Working in Tandem." *Nursing Times: NT* 86 (11 July 1990): 72-73.

   McDowall urges the use of job sharing to "attract, retain, and motivate midwives." She explains a typical midwifery shared schedule and describes some long-term benefits sharers may enjoy.

443. McGuire, Nan, and Suzanne Smith. *Survey of Private Sector Work and Family Policy: San Francisco and Alameda Counties.* San Francisco: New Ways to Work, 1986. 47p.

   Responses from 186 firms that were queried on the availability of several different work-time options (flextime, compressed workweek, permanent part-time, job sharing, and work sharing) are presented in this document. Job sharing was available at 12 percent of the companies in San Francisco County and 13 percent of the companies in Alameda County. A copy of the survey instrument with summary responses is included.

444. Meager, Nigel. "Job Sharing and Job Splitting: Employer Attitudes." *Employment Gazette* 96 (July 1988): 383-388.

Information in this article is drawn from an Institute of Manpower Studies report that surveyed thirty organizations. Slightly over half (sixteen) organizations used job sharing and/or job splitting, which is described along with employers' reasons for implementing job sharing/splitting and their perceived advantages and disadvantages of the issue.

445. Melick, Margaret A. "A Survey of Responses to the Issue of Job Sharing as an Employment Option for Professionals and Para-Professionals in the Dunn County Area." M.S. thesis, University of Wisconsin–Stout, 1978. 75p.

This researcher measured the preference for job sharing as an employment option at professional and para-professional levels by surveying married residents–spouses of University of Wisconsin (Stout) faculty and administrative staff–living in the Dunn County area. Eight employers in the same area with a workforce of more than twenty professional and para-professional employees were also interviewed to see if they used job sharing as a work option. Tables and charts detail the respondents' attitudes toward job-sharing plans and employer benefits for full- and part-time employees. Included in the appendix is "An Employer's Guide to Job Sharing: A New Concept in Dunn County." Bibliography.

446. Meltz, Noah M., Frank Reid, and Gerald S. Swartz. *Sharing the Work: An Analysis of the Issues in Worksharing and Jobsharing.* Toronto: University of Toronto Press, 1981. 90p.

The authors define the difference between work sharing and job sharing. Their intent was to design a theoretical model for Canadian businesses to assess the possibilities and implications of employment sharing (work sharing, job sharing, and part-time employment). Bibliography.

447.   M[icheli], R[obin]. "Two Who Live Better Than One." *Money* 17 (Fall 1988): 81.

Two professional women fulfill their desire to work and also spend time with their babies by sharing a job and a baby-sitter. Each works three days per week with a one-day overlap. They each collect 60 percent of their former salary, full benefits, and half the annual bonuses.

448.   Montgomery, Sheila, Tony O'Reilly, and T. L. Chambers. "Part-Time Work: One Year's Job Share in Bristol." *British Medical Journal* 289 (3 November 1984): 1240-1241.

Physicians who needed to work part-time and who wanted more experience applied for and obtained a shared senior position in pediatrics. This article reports on their experience, the expected and unexpected problems, and administrative arrangements in addition to the organization of their clinical work.

449.   Moorman, Barbara. *Upgrading Part-Time Work: Why Unions Should Support Voluntary Job Sharing*. San Francisco: New Ways to Work, 1982. 13p.

This pamphlet argues for union support of voluntary job sharing. Arguments include these: employees want to job share, it upgrades part-time employment while contributing to full employment, it can be used to help organize unions, and sharers would be good union members.

450.   Nelson-Horchler, Joani. "Derailing the Mommy Track." *Industry Week* 239 (6 August 1990): 22-26.

Part-time employment and job sharing allow many career women to take time off for their children and also to maintain a work schedule that leads to promotions and top corporate positions.

451.   Nelton, Sharon. "Six Ways to Be 'Family-Friendly'." *Nation's Business* 77 (March 1989): 12-13.

A married couple with four children shares the post of assistant chief of the Washington bureau of the *St. Louis Post-Dispatch*. Their managing editor says it works very well.

Nelton includes a list of six ways a company can help its employees balance their time between work and home.

452. "Never on Wednesday." *Law Society's Gazette* (London), 4 December 1985, 3537.

Job sharing and part-time employment for women solicitors was one of the topics under discussion at the 1985 annual conference of London's Law Society. Job sharers said their determination to succeed and their ability to meet their clients' demands alleviated fears of their employers.

453. "New York State Attorney General Takes a Firm Stand on Job Sharing." *BusinessLink* 2 (1986): 9-10.

Included in this article is a description of the job-sharing experiment established in the Office of the New York State Attorney General. Conclusions were that job sharing was feasible and should be made permanent. Brief reports from several businesses in the United States confirm the practicality and the appealing nature of job sharing.

454. "'Nine-Monther' Program Helps Bank, Mothers, and College Students." *ABA Banking Journal* 75 (April 1983): 30-31.

A Boston bank hires mothers to work three-fourths of the year and college students to work the summer months. In addition, they hired two mothers to share the daily duties of a nine-month receptionist position. (See item No. 460 for a related article.)

455. Oakley, Robin, and Clive Edwards. "New Jobs by the Million." *Daily Mail* (London), 27 November 1984, 18-19.

This article includes several shorter reports that investigate unemployment issues in Britain and includes a story on job sharing. Two workers share a position at GEC Telecommunications in Coventry, which allows one of them to train for the Olympics in her spare time.

456. Olson, Jan. "The Part-Time Solution." *Marketing & Media Decisions* 23 (April 1988): 106+108.

The author, a former media planner and job sharer for Carmichael Lynch in Minneapolis, explains how she and her partner shared the work load and the responsibilities to their clients as well as responsibilities to their organization.

457. Oswald, Rosalind. "The Job-Sharing Solicitor." *Law Society's Gazette* (London), 23 April 1986, 1199-1200.

Oswald outlines three steps in setting up a job-sharing plan. These include finding the right partner, deciding how the work will be shared, and making it acceptable to employers and colleagues at work.

458. "Part-Timers, Job Sharers Laid Off at Four Phase." *Work Times* 3 (Winter 1985): 7.

Four Phase, a California-based hi-tech company, decides to discharge several part-time workers including two women who shared the full-time position of personnel recruiter.

459. "Permanent Reduction in Work Hours." In *Work Sharing Case Studies*, by Maureen E. McCarthy and Gail S. Rosenberg. Kalamazoo, MI: W.E. Upjohn Institute for Employment Research, 1981, pp. 129-160.

McCarthy and Rosenberg examine work sharing in several businesses. Descriptions are given of companies that have chosen to reduce work hours in a variety of ways, including job sharing. These pages detail accounts of job sharing in the State of Wisconsin, the Madison, Wisconsin, Public Library, Hewlett-Packard, TRW Vidar, and Black & Decker in addition to the State of California.

460. Perry, Nancy J. "Nine-Month Jobs at Shawmut Bank: A New Version of Job Sharing Attracts Working Mothers." *World of Work Report* 8 (January 1983): 5-6.

Boston's Shawmut Bank allows some of its employees to work nine months of the year. These positions are filled by working parents who want summers off. One drawback to the plan is that these employees are considered part-time and do not receive paid vacations, sick days, or health insurance benefits. (See item No. 454 for a related article.)

461. Pesek, James G., and Charles McGee. "An Analysis of Job Sharing, Full-Time, and Part-time Work Arrangements: One

Hospital's Experience." *American Business Review* 7 (June 1989): 34-40.

Following a general review of job sharing, the authors describe a job-sharing program that began in 1980 at the Brookville, Pennsylvania, Hospital. Included is an analysis of a survey they completed of the full-time, part-time, and job-sharing staff at the hospital. Each group was asked questions about its satisfaction with work schedules, the opportunity for growth or advancement, and job significance. Bibliography.

462. Phillips, Kathryn. "Beyond the Fringes." *New Age Journal* (December 1984): 53-56.

Male co-editors of a weekly newspaper in Berkeley, California, share their job. Each works twenty-five hours a week and receives full health-care benefits. Both enjoy the free time for travel and family that job sharing allows them. They did, however, run into resistance to the idea when a new supervisor was hired.

463. Pinder-Crawford, Ruth, and Lonna M. Nauman. "Job Sharing." *National Shorthand Reporter* 47 (April 1986): 30-31.

Court reporters for a sixteen-county circuit in Iowa share a job. The two women involved enjoy the flexibility of their work in terms of time, task, and location. Neither feels overwhelmed by the amount of transcribing work nor by the amount of time spent away from home.

464. "Rare Newspaper Arrangement: Two Working Mothers to Share Food Editor's Post Temporarily." *Editor & Publisher* 123 (28 April 1990): 44.

The *Contra Costa Times* in northern California decided to allow two temporary employees to share editing responsibilities for its weekly food section while the food editor was on maternity leave. The newspaper has been experimenting with job sharing on a case-by-case basis.

465. "A Real Alternative to Full Employment, with No Catches." *IPM Digest* (Institute of Personnel Management) 209 (December 1982): 9-10.

Leonard Grice, personnel director at GEC Telecommunications, reports some opposition to job sharing from those who think there must be a catch to it. Young people, however, want to job share at GEC, where it is encouraged.

466.   Reid, Helen. "Job Share Duo Double the Skills." *Western Daily Press* (Bristol, England), 30 June 1987, unnumbered.

Aircall, a communications firm in Bristol, England, employees two women to share its office-manager position. Daily work is not split because they work alternate weeks beginning on Wednesdays, which means each is on call every other weekend.

467.   Renfroe, Charles. "Options at ARCO." *Work Times* 2 (March 1984): 1-2.

The director of the Atlantic Richfield Company's senior worker policy and programs division answers questions about retirement plans as well as job-sharing policies for older employers in his organization.

468.   Richmond, Caroline. "Happy Together." *General Practitioner* (4 June 1982): 28.

Women surgeons share a practice but count as one doctor in a five-doctor clinic. The surgeons divide the weekly work schedule and nights on-call. The other doctors as well as the patients are pleased with the job-sharing arrangement.

469.   Rosow, Jerome M., and Robert Zager. "Punch Out the Time Clocks." *Harvard Business Review* 61 (March-April 1983): 12-14+16+20+22+26+28+30.

Rosow and Zager report that changes in lifestyles and work environments have made alternative work schedules a viable option for both employers and employees. They explain how flextime, permanent part-time, job sharing, compressed workweeks, and work sharing can meet the changing personal and professional needs of workers and the demands put on managers to "get the work done." Bibliography.

470. Roszsnyai, Jean. "Job Sharing for Chemists--Can It Work?" *Vortex* (Northern California American Chemical Society) 39 (June 1978): 14.

Traditionally, chemists have not been employed part-time. However, the author points out that employers could gain from hiring a "two-headed" chemist. Positive benefits include job flexibility, alternatives to layoffs, affirmative action compliance, and access to a larger talent pool.

471. Saltzman, Amy. "One Job, Two Contented Workers." *U.S. News & World Report* 105 (14 November 1988): 74+76.

After a month's worth of research and planning, advertising saleswomen for the *Seattle Weekly* proposed job sharing to their employer. Being good salespeople, their strategy included the following: sharers would suffer less burnout, be more efficient, stay with the organization longer, and continue on the job when one partner was off. In addition, they noted job sharing would advance the organization's progressive image.

472. Seal, Kathy. "Job Sharing Finds Share of Interested Users." *Hotel & Motel Management* 206 (23 September 1991): 1+66.

Workers in the American hotel industry are beginning to share jobs. Two women in Chicago share the job of director of national catering accounts for the Marriott Corporation. At the Westin Hotel in Edmonton, Alberta, the position of convention services manager is shared. The salary and vacation time are split but both employees receive benefits (medical, dental, and optical). Although skeptical at first, hotel management personnel agree the shared positions work well.

473. "Sharing Jobs and Satisfaction." *Management Review* 66 (July 1977): 9.

Alza Pharmaceutical Company in Palo Alto, California, institutes job sharing by restructuring its full-time receptionist position. A motivating factor was the difficulty the company had in relieving the regular receptionist for a lunch break.

474. Sherman, Jill. "Nurses Work at Job Share Plan." *Times* (London), 11 June 1987, 3.

An experimental job-sharing arrangement is established by two ward sisters at Charing Cross Hospital in west London. A review of the project by a freelance researcher indicates it was a success due to the nurses' efforts.

475. "Steelcase Offers Job Sharing to the Entire Workforce." *BusinessLink* 4 (1988): 6-7.

After experimenting with job sharing on a limited basis, Steelcase, an office furniture manufacturer in Grand Rapids, Michigan, extended job-sharing opportunities to all its employees. Teams work with the personnel office to arrange schedules and benefits. All employees, including sharers, are eligible for merit raises and seniority promotions.

476. "Steelcase Showcases Job Sharing." *Work Times* 4 (Fall 1985): 1-2.

White-collar workers are employed in job-sharing positions at Steelcase, an office furniture manufacturer in Grand Rapids, Michigan. Evaluations found job sharing to be beneficial to both employees and the company.

477. Sykes, Kay. "Job Splitting in the Office." *Industrial and Commercial Training* 12 (July 1980): 274-275.

Sykes gives reasons why offices should make use of a flexible workforce, which often means hiring permanent part-timers and workers who split a job. The use of temporary workers fills a need for short-term employees but should not be used continually as a replacement for hiring permanent part-time staff.

478. "Take This Job and Share It." *Executive Female* 14 (November/ December 1991): 28.

Steelcase, a Grand Rapids, Michigan, furniture company has in the past allowed its employees to job share with one exception—employees at the professional/managerial level. Two managers (women), whose jobs were to recruit senior designers, propose to the company that they be allowed to share one position. The company agreed and for five years the couple has received praise from both supervisors and clients. Two years ago, they were promoted to senior employment representative.

They both work two-and-a-half days a week and receive half the salary and benefits.

479.   "They Try Job Sharing." *Post-Standard* (Syracuse, NY), 31 March 1981, D5.
After hearing about a job-sharing arrangement in Merrimack Valley, Massachusetts, two elementary school teachers seeking career changes decide to share a position at the General Hospital in Lowell, Massachusetts, working with alcohol abuse patients.

480.   Thomas, Edward G. "Flexible Work Keeps Growing." *Management World* 15 (April/May 1986): 43-45.
A 1985 Administrative Management Society survey reports more companies in the United States are using flextime and job-sharing programs than in 1981.

481.   _____. "Flextime Doubles in a Decade." *Management World* 16 (April/May 1987): 18-19.
Thomas reports that a 1987 Administrative Management Society survey revealed that the number of firms allowing flextime is steadily increasing while the number allowing job sharing has remained about the same since 1985.

482.   _____. "Update on Alternative Work Methods." *Management World* 11 (January 1982): 30-32.
The author compares flextime and job-sharing figures between 1978 and 1981 on surveys conducted by the Administrative Management Society. He also includes examples of how job-sharing workers are compensated.

483.   _____. "Workers Who Set Their Own Time Clocks." *Business and Society Review* (Spring 1987): 49-51.
A review of how job sharing has grown in popularity since the early 1980s is included in this article along with details on flextime scheduling.

484.   "Two Employees for the Price of One." *Personal Report for the Executive* 3 (12 April 1977): 1-3.
Benefits employers can gain from job sharing as well as ways to establish a shared position are listed in this article.

485. "Two Stanford Nurses Develop Unusual Approach to Job."
     Campus Report (Stanford University), 29 October 1980, 11.
     With the approval of their boss, heart transplant Stanford
     Medical Center nurses have been job sharing for several years.
     The sharers recommend it for others, providing it is "a mutual
     decision between two people who know and trust each other."

486. Warnick, Sarah. "Job Sharing Gets Mixed Reviews at California
     Dailies." *Editor & Publisher* 122 (5 August 1989): 22.
     While job sharers at different California newspapers enjoy
     the benefits of a flexible schedule, they also recognize some
     drawbacks. It is often hard to contact sources, develop a long-
     range project, or work on stories in detail. Also, part-timers do
     not receive health benefits and there can be scheduling problems
     in the office.

487. Willis, Judith. "2 Women Become 1 Attorney." *Minneapolis*
     (MN) *Star*, 26 November 1980, C1+C2.
     Women prosecutors in the Hennepin County Public
     Defender's office take the position that they are interchangeable.
     They alternate schedules by working one week on, one week off.

488. Wollman, Jane. "Double-Duty Dentists." *Working Woman* 9
     (March 1984): 147-148.
     Identical female twins who happen to be married to identical
     twins share a dental practice. By planning their pregnancies,
     they also share child care and the nursing of their babies. Each
     dentist practices two days a week and alternating Saturdays.
     They each have their own patients and only substitute for one
     another during dental or personal emergencies.

489. Woodward-Smith, Mary Ann, and Georgia Ridgeway Carruth.
     "Job Sharing: An Alternative Work Pattern for Nurses." *Nursing
     Management* 17 (June 1986): 29-31.
     The authors are nurses who shared a job (clinical specialist)
     at the Veterans Administration Medical Center in Nashville,
     Tennessee, for six months. Before their job-sharing position
     ended, the nurses asked their staff to evaluate the arrangement by
     listing both the positive and negative aspects of the experience
     on a six-item questionnaire. Seventy-two percent of the 67

percent who returned the questionnaire responded positively. Thus, the authors concluded that their experiment was a success and that job sharing was a viable option for nurses. Bibliography.

490. "Work Time Options, Work for the Disabled." *Work Times* 7 (Fall 1988): 1+7.

     In order to help the disabled, Blue Cross/Blue Shield in St. Louis, Missouri, offers job-sharing opportunities to recovering psychiatric patients. Workers who live at the Independence Center of St. Louis are provided with a low-stress entry or reentry position.

491. Young, James R. "How We've Made Job Sharing Work in Our Office." *Medical Economics* 64 (19 January 1987): 47.

     A family practitioner explains how he and his partner hire six part-time employees (three nurses and three secretaries), all of whom work a flexible schedule and can switch with each other when necessary.

492. Zippo, Mary. "Job Sharing: A Way to Avoid Layoffs?" *Personnel* 59 (March-April 1982): 58-60.

     United Airlines instituted job sharing as an alternative to proposed layoffs. It was called "partnership time-off." Participants were responsible for finding their own partners, developing a schedule/salary/benefit plan, and covering for each other when necessary. Vacation and sick leave were to accrue at a half-time rate but the company would continue health insurance, life insurance, and pensions for each.

Education

493. "Action Exchange." *American Libraries* 16 (March 1985): 146-147.

   In answer to a question about job sharing in reference positions, three academic librarians describe how it works, how benefits are split, and how it is accepted by the library administration.

494. *Advice to Members: Job Sharing.* London: The Library Association, 1989. [6p.].

   Supporting the practice of job sharing, this pamphlet identifies types of employees who would be interested in job sharing and answers general questions of both sharers and employers.

495. Alvarado, Yolanda. "City Schools 'Job-Share' Plan May Lessen Teacher Layoffs." *Lansing* (MI) *State Journal*, 13 February 1981, A1+A3.

   Teachers in the Lansing, Michigan, School District are offered job-sharing positions as a way of reducing layoffs.

496. Anderson, Ann M. "Job Sharing at the Winchester Public Library." *News Bulletin* (Boston Chapter, Special Libraries Association) 42 (May/June 1976): 48.

   The author identifies several positions--from professional library assistant to library aide--at the Winchester, Massachusetts, Public Library that are shared by two or, in one case, three people.

497. Anderson, Ian. "Two into One Will Go--with a Bit of a Push." *Guardian* (London), 20 January 1981, 11.

The author encourages the British education secretary and others to try job sharing in their schools. He includes reasons why job sharing will work and provides examples from California schools as well as schools in the United Kingdom.

498.   Angell, Marilyn. "Shared Job Gives Double Satisfaction." *Scottsdale (AZ) Daily Progress*, 25 June 1980, 15.

Two teachers at Ottawa University College Without Walls in Phoenix, Arizona, relate their job-sharing experiences in teaching an introductory course about the university.

499.   Angier, Margaret M. *Job Sharing in Schools: An Account of a Policy in Practice*. Sheffield, England: Sheffield City Polytechnic Department of Education Management, 1984. 91p.

The Sheffield City Council provides the impetus for job sharing in the Sheffield educational system. After its initiation, a study was conducted through questionnaires and interviews with the administrators, job sharers, and the staff in the schools to examine how job sharing was operating and how it was viewed by those involved. Bibliography.

500.   Anthony, Margaret. "Job Sharing: An All Win Situation." *CABE Journal* (Connecticut Association of Boards of Education) (Winter 1985): 8.

Advantages to job-sharing teachers are included in this article. Also provided is a job-sharing policy that could be presented to any board of education.

501.   Arkin, William, and Lynne R. Dobrofsky. "Shared Labor and Love: Job-Sharing Couples in Academia." *Alternative Lifestyles* 1 (November 1978): 492-512.

This article reports the findings of a study undertaken by the authors of fifty-eight job-sharing couples in academia. In addition to surveying the couples, deans of faculty at the forty-two colleges and universities where the couples were employed were surveyed. Responses are categorized by couple, female, male, and employer perceptions. Bibliography.

502.   "At Fillmore, Principal Is Actually Two Women." *Washington Post*, 26 December 1977, A11.

Reasons for sharing a school principalship are given by the two women who share this GS-9 position.

503. Baird, Nancy. "Two for the Price of One." *Kentucky Library Association Bulletin* 44 (Winter 1980): 9-11.

Two reference librarians at Kentucky's Owensboro-Daviess County Public Library share a position. In addition to sharing duties and making joint decisions, each librarian has a list of specific duties.

504. Barrow, Evelyn, and Esther Rothstein. "Harmonious Job Sharing." *School Library Journal* 28 (August 1982): 2-3.

Two school librarians describe the benefits the school district has enjoyed since they began sharing a library position in March 1968.

505. Bayliss, Sarah. "Job Sharing: The Case for Half-Time Work." *Times Educational Supplement* (London), 19 March 1982, 8.

Sheffield, England, teachers are encouraged by job-sharing opportunities even though teachers unions have not thoroughly endorsed the concept. Teachers describe the practicality of job sharing and why they think it is a good idea.

506. _____. "Sheffield to Try Job-Sharing Scheme for Teaching Staff." *Times Educational Supplement* (London), 20 November 1981, 1.

Job sharing is being offered to teachers and staff in Sheffield, England, where it is considered an alternative to a part-time contract.

507. "Benefit from Job Sharing." *Updating School Board Policies* (National School Boards Association) 14 (December 1983): 4.

School systems are discovering that job sharing is a benefit to them, their teachers, and their students. With advanced planning, teachers and school boards will know what is expected of them when a job-sharing program is established.

508. Bennetts, Sandra L. "Job Sharing in the Elementary School: A Minnesota Case Study." M.S. thesis, St. Cloud State University, 1982. 106p.

This thesis tested the hypothesis that shared teaching is a viable alternative to the traditional single-teacher classroom. Two fourth-grade classes at an elementary school in Minnesota were studied during the 1979-80 academic year. Students, parents, teacher colleagues, and administrators were surveyed. Bibliography.

509. Bergmann, Martha. "Job Sharing." *Booklegger Magazine* 1 (1974): 44-46.

Librarians at the San Francisco Public Library were questioned about whether they favored job sharing and if they would apply for it. Negative responses of employers are given as well as advantages seen by two librarians who share a position in a community college library. Bibliography.

510. Blount, Paul. *Job Sharing in Academic Libraries: An Examination of Principles and Practice.* Brighton, England: Council of Polytechnic Librarians, 1991. 67p.

Blount surveyed (via telephone) seventy-three university and polytechnic libraries in England and Scotland to see if they allowed job sharing. While the majority indicated they did not, twenty-three libraries said that they did allow job sharing. The author describes the advantages and disadvantages in addition to the law regarding hours to be worked and statutory rights of employment. He also details the attitudes, policies, and guidelines of trade unions (Association of University Teachers, NALGO, etc.), professional bodies (Library Association, Institute of Personnel Management, etc.), other organizations such as New Ways to Work, and government departments, including the Department of Employment. Specific law cases dealing with anti-discrimination legislation are also detailed as well as ways of insuring successful job-sharing arrangements and examples of other flexible work patterns appropriate for academic libraries. Bibliography.

511. Bobay, Julie. "Job Sharing: A Survey of the Literature and a Plan for Academic Libraries." *Journal of Library Administration* 9 (1988): 59-69.

Included in this article is a general overview of job sharing that ends with the author encouraging academic library administrators to institute and support job-sharing opportunities. Bibliography.

512. Branam, Linda McMahan. "Job Sharing: Attitudes among Elementary School Teachers." Ed.Sp. thesis, University of Tennessee, Knoxville, 1981. 72p.

Nineteen randomly selected school systems within the East Tennessee Development District were surveyed through the use of questionnaires to determine the current attitudes of classroom teachers toward job sharing. Bibliography.

513. Braudy, Judith, and Susan Tuckerman. "The Part-Time Academic Librarian: Current Status, Future Directions." *Library Journal* 111 (1 April 1986): 38-41.

Job sharing is a way for the academic librarian to enjoy part-time work and still take advantage of the opportunities for advancement, permanent positions, and prorated benefits. Bibliography.

514. Buder, Leonard. "Two Teachers Are Better Than None." *New York Times*, 21 May 1967, E7.

A partnership-teaching program is organized by the Women's Educational and Industrial Union in Boston to employ teachers who have been out of the field for a time and who wish to return to teaching on a part-time basis.

515. Burrington, G. A. "Report on the Symposium on Job Sharing in Libraries." *State Librarian. Journal of the Circle of State Librarians* 30 (November 1982): 41-42.

This article reports on a symposium at the Department of Library and Information Studies at Manchester Polytechnic in England in November 1981. Reports were given by job sharers at the Equal Opportunities Commission, an administrator at the Oldham Borough Library, and an employee of the TUC Pensions Department.

516. Cameron, Kenneth Frederick. "The Effects of Selected Social, Demographic and Attitudinal Characteristics and the Preferences Expressed by Teachers for Strategies Intended to Reduce Redun-

dancy and Layoffs." Ph.D. diss., University of Toronto, 1984. 310p.

This dissertation studied New Brunswick teachers' attitudes toward various strategies (retraining, early retirement, job sharing, and a variety of leave plans) that school systems are implementing in order to reduce the need for staff layoffs. The author also explored demographic and attitudinal variables to explain why teachers preferred a particular strategy.

517.   Caplan, Sorrell, and Dorie Caplan. "Job Sharing Helps Teachers, Administrators, and Students." *American School Board Journal* 168 (October 1981): 33-34+42.

School administrators cite reasons for the improvement of education via job sharing. Teachers report compatibility and communication are essential.

518.   Carter, Don. "Sharing Marriage, Jobs." *Seattle Post-Intelligencer*, 15 January 1978, F3.

Two married university history professors share one teaching position at the University of Puget Sound in Tacoma, Washington.

519.   Carter, Sarah, and Frances Hinton. "Job Sharing: A Personal Account." *Librarians for Social Change* 9 (1981): 25-26.

An important advantage of job sharing to these two behavioral science librarians at the University of Kent was that one could pick up the other's work at any time. By overlapping some work time, policies and new subjects could be discussed as well as new methods of instruction.

520.   Dapper, Gloria. "Half-Time Teachers." *Instructor* 79 (November 1969): 87-88.

Partnership teaching is used at the elementary level in Framingham, Massachusetts. The partnership-teaching program began here under the guidance of the Women's Educational and Industrial Union of Boston. Principals have found part-time teachers to be well-prepared—usually because they are concentrating on their specialties.

521. Davidson, Wilma, and Susan Kline. "How to Get Two Experienced Teachers–for the Price of One." *American School Board Journal* 164 (September 1977): 35-36.

Two high school English teachers not only share the classroom at Minnechaug Regional High School in Wilbraham, Massachusetts, but also share child care. They believe the key ingredients to making it work are compromise and a sense of commitment.

522. _____. "Job Sharing for Teachers." *Working Woman* 2 (June 1977): 61.

The authors tout their job-sharing arrangement and say it fits nicely into the public school schedule. They each teach high school English classes and fulfill extra-help duties such as study hall and meeting individually with students on a one-to-one basis.

523. _____. "Job Sharing in Education." *Clearing House* 52 (January 1979): 226-228.

Davidson and Kline point out several places where job sharing is working. They give reasons why administrators are just as comfortable with job sharing as teachers. Bibliography.

524. "Declining Enrollment: Job Sharing Is One Answer." *California School Boards* 35 (May 1976): 10-11.

Nine San Francisco area school districts have job sharing. Both instructors and administrators feel the advantages outweigh the disadvantages.

525. "Delegates Like Idea of Job Sharing." *Irish Times* (Dublin), 8 April 1983, 6.

Irish secondary school teachers approve the concept of job sharing at their annual conference in Blarney, Ireland.

526. Dixon, Beryl. "How Celia and Fiona Found a Job They Could Share." *Times* (London), 17 February 1987, 29.

A research officer position in the House of Commons Library is shared by two women, each of whom works two-and-a-half days a week. British job sharers are entitled to some of the same rights as full-time employees. However, benefits paid to sharers vary greatly.

527. Dombrink, Patricia L. "How One Couple Spends Less Time Working." *Christian Science Monitor*, 8 August 1977, 18.

In order to share in the responsibility of raising their son, a mother job shares in the mornings in an Oakland, California, elementary school, while the father works as a part-time lawyer only in the afternoons.

528. Drake, Marjorie. "Five-Tenths Plus Five-Tenths Equals One Teacher." *Guardian* (London), 11 June 1985, 11.

Primary school teachers feel job sharing is a plus for both teachers and students. Objections are most often raised by school administrators and union officials who are concerned about the lack of security and the erosion of benefits.

529. _____. "Job Sharing." *Christian Woman* (British ed.) (October 1985): 28-29+31.

Part-time employment carries several connotations—poor pay, low regard, and limited prospects for promotion—that many workers wish to avoid. Drake describes several couples who deal with these problems by job-sharing positions in which they experience opportunities for advancement, better salaries, and part-time work they enjoy.

530. Early, Maureen. "Job Sharing: An Idea Whose Time Has Come." *Newsday* (Long Island, NY), 29 July 1980, Part II, 8+9.

Career counselors at New York's Marymount Manhattan College share a position while one spends her free time pursuing her own business and the other takes care of her family. Included in this article are reasons why job sharing is not the same as permanent part-time employment.

531. Edwards, Viv, and Jenny Cheshire. "Two into One Will Go—with Suitable Adjustments." *Guardian* (London), 4 September 1980, 10.

Sharers in the Linguistics Department at Reading University recount their experiment of replacing someone on a year's leave of absence. Covering for each other at work and sharing child-care duties turned out to be more work than either teacher had expected.

532. *Evaluation of Job Sharing in the Department of Education: Tenured Employee Pairings and Public Librarians.* Honolulu: Office of the Legislative Auditor, 1984. 17p.

Presented in this report is the evaluation of job-sharing teachers in the school systems in Hawaii and the pilot testing of job sharing for public librarians. Recommendations for the future are included.

533. *Evaluation of Job Sharing in the Public Library System.* Honolulu: Office of the Legislative Auditor, 1986. 9p.

After guidelines were established for job-sharing teachers in Hawaii, public librarians were given the opportunity to participate in job sharing. This report evaluates the costs, benefits, and participation of fourteen library workers who took part in the experiment.

534. *Evaluation of the Job Sharing Pilot Project in the Department of Education.* Honolulu: Office of the Legislative Auditor, 1980. 39p.

This report presents the results of the job-sharing pilot project that was implemented in Hawaii's Department of Education during the 1979 spring semester. Interviews were conducted with 120 teachers who participated in the project in order to gather demographic characteristics of the job sharers. Principals as well as a randomly selected sample of elementary students and their parents were also interviewed. Summaries are included on the program's effectiveness, costs (administrative and operating), and issues. Recommendations follow.

535. Forbes, Shari. "Beaverton Teachers Share Jobs." *Oregon Education* 57 (May 1983): 6.

After thirteen years of full-time teaching, two elementary teachers at Chehalem Elementary School in Beaverton, Oregon, begin to share one position. They keep a detailed notebook and a common plan book in addition to communicating over the phone and during lunch recess once a week.

536.   Furey, James P., and Steven R. Heilbronner. "Sharing a Job in Schaumburg, Illinois." *Phi Delta Kappan* 67 (February 1986): 468.

An elementary school district in Schaumburg, Illinois, offers job sharing to tenured teachers. Salary, seniority, insurance, sick leave, and retirement benefits are based on percentage of time worked.

537.   Gallese, Liz Roman. "Colleges Say They Get More for Their Money by Hiring a Couple to Share One Faculty Job." In *Careers and Couples: An Academic Question*, edited by Leonore Hoffmann and Gloria DeSole. New York: Modern Language Association of America, 1976, pp. 42-44.

Cited below as item No. 538.

538.   _____. "Colleges Say They Get More for Their Money by Hiring a Couple to Share One Faculty Job." *Wall Street Journal*, 19 April 1974, 30.

Colleges across the U.S. are employing job-sharing couples. In addition to getting more for their money, college administrators see job sharing as a way of recruiting more female faculty members. Procedures must be specified regarding tenure decisions.

539.   Galloway, Gail R. "Part-Time Teaching and Job Sharing in Georgia's Public Schools: A Status Report." Ph.D. diss., Georgia State University, 1990. 131p.

This researcher defines job-sharing teachers as permanent part-time employees. Through the use of a written survey sent to the superintendents or personnel directors in all the public schools in Georgia, Galloway was able to report on the status of part-time teaching in that state. She followed this with direct surveys (to collect demographic data) to the part-time teachers. She later conducted telephone interviews (for attitudinal data) with a sample of the part-timers who had returned their personal surveys. Detailed results and conclusions are included in this dissertation as well as copies of all the questionnaires and letters to administrators and teachers. Bibliography.

540. Garman, Dorothy. *The Effects of Job Sharing on Student Performance; Literature Review.* Glen Ellyn, IL: The Institute for Educational Research, 1988. 5p. ERIC, ED 300 337.

Garman reports that a search of the ERIC database revealed few publications that address the topic of student performance and job sharing among school personnel. Her literature review summarizes what she found—mostly anecdotal reports of the impact job sharing has on students. She found students were less likely to be surveyed than teachers and administrators. Bibliography.

541. Gilbert, Cecily, and Kathleen Gray. "Job Sharing in a Hospital Library." *Australian Special Library News* 18 (June 1985): 51+53-55.

These two authors define job sharing, give examples of where in Australia shared jobs can be found, cite pros and cons of job sharing, and relate their experiences of sharing a librarian position in a hospital. They felt an "immediate boost in morale and productivity." Included also is information on how they implemented the job-sharing arrangement, how they communicated, how the work load was divided, and how decisions were made. Bibliography.

542. Goddard, Catriona. "Job Sharing in British Libraries: Implications for the Manager." *Journal of Librarianship and Information Science* 23 (December 1991): 191-201.

Goddard defines and explains what job sharing is, what it involves, and ways to implement it in addition to where and why individuals are job sharing. She details its advantages and disadvantages by focusing on the manager's viewpoint. She also discusses the legal implications of job sharing as well as answering the question "Do employees have a legal right to job share?"

543. "Going 50-50." *Personnel* 53 (May-June 1976): 8-9.

Job-sharing experiments for California teachers in the San Francisco Bay area schools have been successful. Advantages found by Gretl Meier include more diversity among teachers, retention of senior teachers, and acceptable alternatives to cutbacks and layoffs.

544. Goodburn, Edna. "Two for the Plight of One." *Junior Education*
      5 (June 1981): 11.
      The administrator of the Swinley County Primary School in
      Berkshire, England, supports job sharing in the classroom. Job
      sharing works best if the partners share the same philosophy as
      well as practical aspects of keeping joint records and
      communicating daily.

545. Gordon, Pamela, and B. J. Meadows. "Sharing a Principalship:
      When Two Heads Are Better Than One." *Principal* 66
      (September 1986): 26-29.
      Setting a precedent, two women who both wanted to pursue
      doctorates in higher education try sharing the principalship at
      Normandy Elementary School (a year-round school) in Jefferson
      County, Colorado. In order to convince their superintendent,
      they worked out a management proposal that listed several
      advantages and included their schedule of two months on, two
      months off. Evaluations of parents, colleagues, and administra-
      tors were positive. Bibliography.

546. Greenbaum, Roger. "Job Sharing." *Louisville* (KY) *Times*, 18
      October 1977, C1.
      Louisville, Kentucky's YWCA and Jefferson High School
      both employ job sharers. The teachers each meet three English
      classes a day and substitute for one another when necessary.
      The YWCA employees share the position of job placement
      counselor and also share the salary, vacation time, and sick
      leave.

547. Groner, Alex, and Carlyn Brall. "Part-Time Teachers." *Today's
      Education* 59 (January 1970): 64-65.
      In 1965, the New York organization Catalyst identified
      several states where school systems were employing part-timers.
      They included Florida, Iowa, Massachusetts, Michigan, and
      New York. The schools in Framingham, Massachusetts, coined
      the phrase "partnership teaching"--two teachers sharing one full-
      time position.

548. *Guide to Policies and Contracts on Job Sharing in the Schools.*
      San Francisco: New Ways to Work, 1980. 38p.

This guide was written to assist school districts, teachers' associations, and unions in preparing job-sharing policies and contracts. The application process, pairing, selecting, scheduling as well as compensation, benefits, and returning to full-time employment are all spelled out. Included in the appendix are sample collective bargaining and individual employment contracts in addition to written policies from a selected group of school districts in California.

549. Haar, Gail, and Ami Weber. "Job Sharing." *Connecticut Libraries* 20 (1978): 43-44.

Community services librarians assess their job-sharing position at the Prosser Public Library in Bloomfield, Connecticut. The division of salary and duties, including the rotation of Saturday and evening work with other employees, was jointly determined in consultation with the library director. Communication and personnel benefits have been the hardest problems to deal with.

550. Harris, Lee. "Job Sharing Merits Praised by Teachers." *Los Angeles Times*, 31 May 1984, Section IX, 1+10.

Schools in the Los Angeles area approve of tandem teaching--two teachers sharing the classroom duties of one teacher. Some school districts provide full fringe benefits for both teachers.

551. Hatcher, Jennifer Gwen. "Job Sharing: A Survey of Knowledge and Attitudes of Superintendents toward Partnership Teaching Arrangements." Ph.D. diss., University of Tennessee, Knoxville, 1989. 134p.

Hatcher's investigation of Tennessee school superintendents (ninety-two) is reported in this dissertation. She questioned and analyzed the superintendents' knowledge and attitudes of job sharing in addition to assessing whether job-sharing opportunities were likely to become available in Tennessee schools. The majority of superintendents understood the concept of job sharing and understood the importance of flexibility to many employees. Some, however, did not see job sharing as a viable option and only a few had supervised job sharers. A copy of the survey instrument is included. Bibliography.

552. Henderson, Brian. "Permanent Part-Time Employment and Job Sharing in Library Work." *Australian Special Libraries News* 13 (June 1980): 37-40.

According to the author, the Library Association of Australia has a commitment to the employment practices of job sharing and permanent part-time work. He warns, however, that while people can share responsibilities and tasks, they must have separate contracts of employment.

553. Hendrickson, Barbara. "Job Sharing: An Alternative to Full-Time Teaching." *Learning* 9 (April/May 1981): 34-36.

Two male teachers share a classroom in Oakland, California. Hendrickson identifies reasons for shared teaching and how to get started. She also describes a shared teaching arrangement that was not successful and the reasons for its failure.

554. Hill, Karen. "Life outside the Workplace." *Wilson Library Bulletin* 59 (February 1985): 373.

The Campbell County Public Library located in Gillette, Wyoming, has job-sharing positions in circulation, reference, and the business office.

555. Houston, Jack. "Teachers Testing Job Sharing Waters." *Chicago Tribune*, 16 September 1990, Section 2 (Chicagoland), 1+6.

The Schaumburg, Illinois, Consolidated School District employs eighteen pairs of job sharers. Teachers say they need to have the same teaching style and philosophy to make it work. Administrators see job sharing as a way of helping school districts that face a shortage of qualified teachers. The National Education Association supports job sharing "as long as it's voluntary and is used to provide a flexible job opportunity to help meet the needs of employees."

556. Howell, Jane L. "Job Sharing for Librarians." *News Bulletin* (Boston Chapter, Special Libraries Association) 42 (May/June 1976): 47-48.

Howell describes a survey she conducted while attending the University of Denver Graduate School of Librarianship. She interviewed fifty-five library administrators on the topic of job sharing. One finding pertained to positions most suitable for sharing. These were "thought to be reference and public service, cataloging, and circulation."

557. Hunt, Pauline. "How Splitting Jobs Can Be a Real Education." *Cambridge* (England) *Evening News*, 27 June 1985, 19.

Parkside Community College in England hires art teachers (one man and one woman) to share a teaching position. They meet for three hours each week to discuss the work and make plans.

558. "Husband, Wife Share Job." *Tech Talk* (Massachusetts Institute of Technology) 18 (13 February 1974): 1+3.

A married couple becomes the first couple to share an administrative position at MIT. As co-directors of the Office of Personnel Development, they will each work part-time. This type of arrangement is not new to them because they have previously job shared for several years at other places of employment.

559. Hutton, Clifford E., and Joy Simon McFarlin. "Providing Better University Personnel through Job Sharing." *Journal of the College and University Personnel Association* 33 (Summer 1982): 36-38.

Reasons for the movement toward more flexible hours are included in this article along with an analysis of why job sharing is a successful alternative to rigid work schedules.

560. Jay, Elizabeth. "Boulder Couple Shares a Job." *Town and Country Review* 13 (27 December 1976): 2+12.

At Casey Junior High School in Boulder, Colorado, a married couple shares the duties of teacher-coordinator of the cooperative work experience program. As a team, they have encountered few problems with parents, school staff, or employers of the students.

561. "Job Shared--To Everyone's Benefit." *Teacher's Voice* (Michigan Education Association) 59 (16 November 1981): 16.

Officially approved by the Kalamazoo Education Association, job-sharing contracts provide for prorated salaries, retirement, and medical insurance. School officials believe job sharing saves the district money in addition to reducing the number of teacher layoffs due to decreases in school enrollments.

562. *Job Sharing: An Alternative to Traditional Employment Patterns.* Arlington, VA: Educational Research Service, 1981. 49p.

This publication begins with an overview of job sharing, which is followed by descriptions of various studies conducted by Catalyst, New Ways to Work in San Francisco, and the W.E. Upjohn Institute. The book concludes with examples of job-sharing policies and guidelines from a variety of public school districts. These include the following: Ann Arbor, Michigan; Fremont, California; Honolulu, Hawaii; Louisville, Kentucky; and Wichita, Kansas. Bibliography.

563. "Job Sharing: An Emerging Concept." *AASPA Bulletin* (American Association of School Personnel Administrators) (June 1979): 4+6.

This article reports on Gretl Meier's research (see item No. 204) of 238 workers in job-sharing positions and the 1978 act legislated by the state of Hawaii to establish a three-year job-sharing pilot project. Also included are discussions of problem areas that emerged after the first year of the pilot project.

564. "Job Sharing Answer to Home versus Career." *EDU-GRAM* (Oregon Department of Education) 15 (May 1983): 11.

Two Beaverton, Oregon, school teachers narrate how and why job sharing works for them. Both wanted a career in addition to spending more time with their families. With the support of their principal, they set up a shared schedule and planned a meeting with parents to explain how the shared classroom would work.

565. "Job Sharing Catches On." *Information Legislative Service* (Pennsylvania School Boards Association) 23 (30 August 1985): 16.

Beaverton, Oregon, schools have allowed job sharing for several years and schools in Dearborn, Michigan, are initiating such a program for their teachers.

566. *Job Sharing for Teachers.* Ottawa: Canadian Teachers' Federation, 1985. 30p. ERIC, ED 269 378.

This document focuses on books and articles relating to job sharing for teachers. It contains thirty-seven book citations and ninety-four periodical citations, most of which were written in the late 1970s or early 1980s. Some of the entries are annotated.

567. "Job Sharing for Teachers--A Handbook." In *Report of the Ad Hoc Committee on Part-Time Teachers*, by the Saskatchewan Teachers' Federation. Regina: Saskatchewan Teachers' Federation, 1985, pp. 41-55.

Topics in the "handbook" include the history of job sharing, how to begin, planning the partnership, scheduling, sharing responsibilities, substituting arrangements, implications for principals, the first week of school, and returning to full-time teaching. Also included are quotes from teachers, students, principals, and parents about their feelings toward job sharing. Bibliography.

568. "Job Sharing for Teachers Catches On." *Nation's Schools Report* 2 (29 March 1976): 1- 2.

In addition to alleviating problems with declining enrollments and teacher layoffs, job sharing is seen as an answer to staff stagnation. A survey of nine school districts in the San Francisco area found that only a few had specific policies and procedures for job sharing but that it was very popular with both teachers and administrators.

569. *Job Sharing in ILEA Schools: A Survey of the Pilot Scheme.* London: Inner London Education Authority, 1986. 11p.

This survey reports on the pilot job-sharing project begun in September 1984 for teachers in the Inner London Education Authority (ILEA). Information was collected through interviews and questionnaires. The survey includes details on the type of school, method of appointment, reasons for job sharing, and views of the job sharers as well as their supervisors.

570. "Job Sharing in Libraries: Report from Massachusetts." *Library Journal* 101 (15 November 1976): 2331-2332.

This report summarizes four articles (see item Nos. 94, 496, 556, and 644) on job sharing in libraries which were published in the May/June 1976 issue of the *News Bulletin* of the Boston Chapter of the Special Libraries Association.

571. *Job Sharing in the Schools.* San Francisco: New Ways to Work, 1980. 85p. ERIC, ED 197 088.

Beginning with background information on job-sharing programs in California, Hawaii, and Massachusetts schools, this book continues with a description of why and how job sharing is initiated. Also included is information on the cost and impact it has on education along with reactions from school administrators, parents, and teachers' unions. The appendix includes sample evaluations for parents, principals, teachers, and students.

572. "Job Sharing/Partnership Teaching Discussion Paper Released." *Saskatchewan Bulletin* 47 (28 November 1980): 4-5.

The advantages of partnership teaching are cited along with a chart showing an increase from 1970 to 1980 in the number of part-time teachers in Saskatchewan. Noted also are the limitations of part-time teaching such as restricted benefits. In addition, two examples of partnership teaching are detailed.

573. *Job Sharing Pilot Project.* Honolulu: Department of Education, Office of Personnel Services, 1978. 28p. ERIC, ED 198 298.

This document describes a project that was designed to test the feasibility of job sharing in Hawaii's public schools. Included are descriptions, definitions, selection criteria, procedures, and schedules along with models of teacher request forms, interview assessment sheets, and examples of employee fringe benefits.

574. *Job Sharing Pilot Project.* Rev. ed. Honolulu: Department of Education, Office of Personnel Services, 1981. 21p.

This document revises information contained in the 1978 *Job Sharing Pilot Project.* Hawaii's 1981 state legislature designated the Department of Education to extend its job-sharing project for an additional two years—until 1983. The standard forms and additional information necessary to make that happen are included in this revised document.

575. *Job Sharing Pilot Project in the Department of Education: Final Evaluation.* Honolulu: Office of the Legislative Auditor, 1981. 58p. ERIC, ED 199 531.

This report presents the final evaluation of the State of Hawaii Department of Education's test of job sharing. Chapter titles include these: introduction, background, program effectiveness, program costs, and considerations in establishing job sharing as a permanent employment option.

576. *Job Sharing Pilot Project Procedures for Tenured/New Hire Job Sharing Arrangements.* Honolulu: Department of Education, Office of Personnel Services, 1983. 26p.

Procedures and guidelines are identified in this manual for establishing a job-sharing arrangement between a tenured and non-tenured teacher. Examples of requests for job sharing, agreements for temporary employment, and proposed job-sharing plans (schedules and division of duties) are included.

577. *Job Sharing Pilot Project Procedures for Tenured/Tenured Job Sharing Arrangements.* Honolulu: Department of Education, Office of Personnel Services [1983]. 16p.

This booklet outlines the guidelines and procedures to be followed when two tenured teachers apply for a job-sharing position in Hawaii's public schools. Included are copies of standard forms to be used when requesting job sharing and a chart identifying employee fringe benefits.

578. *Job Sharing Program Procedures.* Honolulu: Department of Education [1991. 23p.].

Hawaii's job-sharing program for teachers began as a pilot project in 1978. This booklet outlines the policies and procedures used for hiring job-sharing teachers. It includes the criteria for selection, application procedures, time schedules, and administrative controls in addition to sample forms to be used by hiring authorities and applicants.

579. Jobbins, David. "Two into One Will Go." *Times Higher Education Supplement* (London), 18 March 1983, 10.
       Opposition to job splitting has been launched by trade union leaders. They point out the necessity of firm guidelines for voluntary job sharing, which has become identified as a women's issue. However, not all women use job sharing to combine career and family responsibilities. For example, two east London female college lecturers use their free time to pursue advanced degrees while retaining the right to return to full-time teaching.

580. "Jobs Sharing--Inconvenient or Common Sense?" *Working for Sheffield* (England) (December 1987): 2.
       Job sharers are employed in various positions in Sheffield. In fact, libraries employ thirty-two job sharers, who see the benefits of sharing versus part-time employment. This article includes positive and negative points for both the worker and the manager.

581. Johnson, Louise, and Lois A. Meerdink. "Job Sharing: An Employment Alternative for the Career Services Professional." *Journal of College Placement* 45 (Winter 1985): 29-30.
       Job sharers at the University of Arizona's career and placement services describe their position, including its advantages, potential problems, client reactions, and reasons for its success. In addition, they relate their schedules, how they communicate, and how they divide benefits.

582. Kay, Jeanne. "Job Sharing in Geography." *Transition* 12 (Summer 1982): 19-22.
       Married geography professors fill one position at the University of Utah. Both were hired in tenure-track positions with full-time health and retirement benefits. Bibliography.

583. Kaye, Cynthia, and Bonnie Williamson. "When It Takes Two to Teach." *Instructor* 95 (May 1986): 50-52.

The authors give tips on how to find a job-sharing partner, classroom rules that must be agreed upon, how to set up a shared schedule, and ways to be supportive of one another when dealing with students, parents, and administrators.

584. "Kings County: Job Sharing Receives Top Marks." *Teacher* (Nova Scotia Teachers Union) 22 (18 January 1984): 9.

Teachers at Cornwallis District High School in Canning, Nova Scotia, were the first in Kings County to engage in job sharing. Both are permanent teachers and can return to full-time status whenever they wish. They each receive half pension but full insurance benefits.

585. Kumar, Krishna. *Job Sharing through Part-Time Contracts: A Consideration in the Context of Declining School Enrollments in Ontario.* Toronto: Commission on Declining School Enrollments in Ontario, 1978. 30p.

This Canadian report describes a study of the attitudes of teachers and school board officials in Ontario toward job sharing in schools. Two questionnaires (copies are included) were used to gather responses, which are detailed along with conclusions and recommendations. Also included is an analysis of the benefits, feasibility of some work arrangements, and implementation problems. Bibliography.

586. Kunkel, Audrey. "Job Sharing Benefits Teachers, Students." *Saskatchewan Bulletin* 49 (4 February 1983): 1-2.

Teachers and school administrators in Regina, Saskatchewan, agree that job sharing can be beneficial to both students and teachers. This article describes various school situations where it has worked and why.

587. Lantz, Mahlon L. "Job Sharing: One District's Experience." *Spectrum: Journal of School Research and Information* 1 (Summer 1983): 23-26.

This article describes the initiation and evaluation of job sharing in the Kalamazoo, Michigan, public schools during the 1979-80 school year. Results of questionnaires to principals, teachers, and parents are included as well as a copy of the contract between the board of education and job-sharing participants. Also included are the procedures used in implementing the job-sharing program.

588.   Laursen, Irene, and Barry Hennessey, eds. *Alternative Work Patterns: Ideas and Experiences; with a Selected Annotated Bibliography.* Boston: Special Libraries Association, 1976. 15p.

This is a collection of nine articles and a bibliography on job sharing, flextime, the four-day workweek, part-time employment, and volunteering in libraries, which has been reprinted by the Boston Chapter of the Special Libraries Association from its May/June 1976 *News Bulletin.* Relevant articles are listed individually in this book.

589.   "Legislative Action Promotes Job Sharing in State Schools." *Bellingham* (WA) *Herald,* 8 October 1989, C1.

A bill passed in the Washington state legislature requires schools "to make job sharing available to certified staff" and to consider all applications received from teachers who want to share one position.

590.   LeNoury, J. "Job Sharing: A Beneficial and Viable Alternative." *Teacher Education* (University of Toronto) (April 1983): 84-100.

In the face of declining enrollments, unemployment, and new technology, this author suggests job sharing as an alternative to layoffs. He identifies who would benefit, what those benefits entail, and problems that are inherent in job sharing. He concludes with two case studies of teachers who are job sharing. Bibliography.

591.   Leone, Marcia. "Job Sharing: An Alternative for Teachers." *Michigan School Board Journal* 31 (July-August 1984): 20+22+24.

This article briefly describes job-sharing programs in California, Hawaii, and Massachusetts. Description of benefits to both teachers and school districts in Michigan are included as well as details that school boards need to be aware of when implementing job-sharing programs.

592. MacWaters, Cristi, Diana Hogarth, Holley Lange, Jane Smith, Diana Wess, Lindsey Wess, and Donlyn Whissen. "Job Sharing: An Option in Colorado Libraries?" *Colorado Libraries* 17 (March 1991): 28-30.

This article is an outgrowth of a committee assignment to explore the idea of job sharing at Colorado State University libraries. A survey of personnel officers revealed little job sharing but considerable interest in it. Included here is an outline for implementing a job-sharing arrangement and reasons why it should be considered a viable work option for university employees. Bibliography.

593. Malcolm, Fiona. "The Couple Who Job Share...A Church!" *Parents* (British ed.) (September 1985): 77-79.

Husband and wife share the calling of running a church in London. This pioneer effort has allowed them both to pursue the profession they want as well as to share in raising their daughter. Their work schedule has been divided by one week on, one week off, and they also share in the cooking and housekeeping duties.

594. Marinelli, Marilyn, and Kathy Berman. "Divide and Conquer-- Everything!" *Supervision* 52 (April 1991): 3-5.

Boulder, Colorado, elementary school principals (women) devised a plan in order to obtain their supervisor's support for job sharing. Their plan outlined the major areas of responsibilities and how they intended to divide them. They discussed the idea with teachers in addition to parents and received interesting feedback, including questions about reduced salaries, job responsibility, and partner compatibility.

595. Marley, Ursula. "Job Sharing: Compatibility, Commitment, Communication and Consistency." *Library Association Record* 92 (March 1990): 197-199.

Difficulties encountered by the author in securing a job-sharing position as a librarian are described in this article. Administrators in the library as well as some staff were opposed to the idea of job sharing but after securing the position, Marley and her partner were able to alleviate most of the staff's fears.

Both try to communicate with each other before making major decisions.

596.   Maroni, Pat. "Two Young Mothers Sharing Single Job." *Tech Talk* (Massachusetts Institute of Technology) (26 June 1974): 1+5.

The dean responsible for the freshman advisory office at the Massachusetts Institute of Technology approves of job sharing and believes the benefits of a four-hour work block outweigh other problems. The women in the position depend on team effort--both at work and at home. While one is working, the other is baby-sitting their children.

597.   "Marriage of the Minds." *Time* 111 (6 March 1978): 68+72.

Despite skepticism on the part of some college administrators, married couples can successfully share one teaching assignment.

598.   Matas, Robert. "Changes in Pension to Foster Job Sharing." *Globe and Mail* (Toronto), 31 August 1983, 4.

In order to help young teachers find part-time jobs and reduce the number of older instructors, Ontario teachers are being encouraged to phase into retirement via job sharing. They can share a teaching position for three years and still contribute to the pension plan as full-time employees.

599.   "May Testifies on Job Sharing." *Action* (Jefferson County Teachers Association, Louisville, KY) (9 October 1979): 1.

The president of the Jefferson County Teachers Association in Louisville, Kentucky, expresses grave reservations about job sharing. Lloyd May feels that because part-timers expect full or proportional benefits they create more employee morale problems than full-timers. Also, he is afraid that some people view teaching as a part-time profession anyway and that job sharing does nothing to dispel that attitude.

600.   McCarthy, Patrice. "Job Sharing." *CABE Journal* (Connecticut Association of Boards of Education) (January-February 1984): 7-8.

Connecticut school administrators believe that a job-sharing proposal should be initiated by teachers who must prove they can work together. Reasons for job sharing and other comments are included in this article from a representative of the Connecticut General Assembly (the chair of its Job Sharing Study Committee) and a job-sharing specialist.

601. McGuire, Helen L. "Opting for Part-Time, or Combining Motherhood with Teaching." *English Journal* 73 (April 1984): 38-40.

After a year's maternity leave, this high school English teacher does not want to give up the time spent with her child during the day. She decides to share her position with another teacher and finds it is a good way to ease into the work routine.

602. McKee, Anna Marie, and Laura Scott. "Job Sharing: A Speech by Patricia Lee and Panel Discussion." *Journal of Library Administration* 3 (Summer 1982): 77-87.

This article is an edited transcript of a speech given by the founder and executive director of Workshare, Inc., Patricia Lee. Job sharing was the topic of discussion at a New Jersey chapter of the Special Libraries Association meeting, and after Lee's speech, a panel of librarians answered questions about job sharing at their institutions. Bibliography.

603. McLachlan, Johanne, and Isabella Trahn. "Job Sharing in an Academic Library." *Australian Library Journal* 30 (August 1981): 77-82.

Librarians at the University of New South Wales discuss personal backgrounds and reasons for choosing job sharing. In addition, they describe how their job works and the benefits they receive. Also included is a list of the advantages and disadvantages of job sharing as seen by their supervisor, the director of the university library. Bibliography.

604. Meikle, James. "Minister to Push for More Job Sharing." *Times Educational Supplement* (London), 26 December 1986, 1.

The British Education Secretary wants to increase part-time employment for women school teachers, especially in the science area. Job sharing is to be encouraged for married women returning to teaching.

605.   Merwin, Elizabeth G., and Sondra Voss. "School Nurses Share a Job." *Journal of School Health* 51 (December 1981): 644-645.

When a school district nurse wanted to phase into retirement, the possibility of creating a job-sharing team was investigated and a nurse who had substituted for the school district was hired. Principals, superintendents, secretaries, teachers, and parents were all queried about the strengths and weaknesses of the program. Advantages and disadvantages as viewed by the nurses are also included. Bibliography.

606.   Metzner, Seymour. "Partnership Teaching: A Remedy for Teacher Turnover in Disadvantaged Areas." *Urban Review* 3 (April 1969): 23.

Partnership teaching is viewed by this author as a way to eliminate some of the stress that is experienced by teachers in large urban areas. It can also be a means of attracting unemployed experienced teachers who have expressed an interest in part-time teaching careers. Bibliography.

607.   Mikitka, Kathleen Faith. "Job-Sharing Couples in Academia: Administrative Policies and Practices." *Journal of the National Association for Women Deans, Administrators, and Counselors* 47 (Spring 1984): 21-27.

For this article, researcher Mikitka undertook a study of twelve four-year institutions and sixteen administrators who have been involved with job sharing from one-to-eight years. Through personal interviews, the author obtained the administrators' views on the impact job sharing has had on the institutions and the implications for the future. Included are items of interest to the job-sharing faculty team--contract models, division of work load, voting, tenure track considerations and probationary periods, qualifications, and performance evaluations in addition to salaries and benefits. Bibliography.

608.   _____. "Spouse-Shared Faculty Appointments: Collegial and Familial Adaptations." Ph.D. diss., Boston College, 1981. 351p.

Investigation of job sharing in colleges and universities in the United States is the subject of this dissertation. Twenty-three married couples and sixteen administrators from twelve institutions of higher education comprised the research sample. Mikitka profiles the couples themselves, gives reasons why couples decide to job share, and describes various employment practices (hiring, salary, tenure, benefits, and leaves) of the academic units. Charts and tables detail the couples' division of labor at home and at work. Bibliography.

609. Mikitka, Kathleen Faith, and Sally A. Koblinsky. "Job-Sharing Couples in Academia: Career and Family Lifestyles." *Home Economics Research Journal* 14 (December 1985): 195-207.

The authors via interviews and written questionnaires investigated twenty couples in job-sharing positions at twelve different four-year colleges. The couples provided information on their reasons for job sharing, their faculty work load, and their division of household duties. The couples were also asked to indicate their degree of satisfaction with their personal, familial, and professional lifestyles. Tables in addition to the text summarize the couples' feelings. Bibliography.

610. Miller, Don. "Job Sharing at the Greater Victoria Public Library." *Canadian Library Journal* 35 (October 1978): 375-377.

Before deciding to implement job sharing at the Greater Victoria Public Library (GVPL) in British Columbia, large public libraries in Canada were surveyed about job-sharing opportunities. Although the results showed limited job-sharing schemes, GVPL decided to try it. This article includes the terms of the pilot project as well as the popular advantages of job sharing as cited by others.

611. Mitchell, Rosella E. "An Evaluation of a Pilot Project in Job Sharing as a Teacher Employment Strategy." M.Ed. thesis, University of Regina, 1986. 136p.

This thesis was designed to study the two-year pilot project of job sharing undertaken in Regina, Saskatchewan. Through telephone/personal interviews, classroom observation, and questionnaires, the researcher collected data on how the job-sharing positions were implemented, how the partners worked together, welfare concerns of the partners, and the attitudes of principals, teachers, and students, as well as parents, toward job sharing in their schools. Copies of the questionnaires are included in the appendices. Bibliography.

612. "Model Collective Bargaining Contract for Job Sharing." *Nation's Schools Report* 6 (29 December 1980): 5.

This is a nine-point statement on job sharing in schools that could be used as a model for a collective bargaining contract.

613. Moorman, Barbara. "Job Sharing: An Administrative View." *Bulletin* (Association of Wisconsin School Administrators) (September 1981): 15-16.

Some administrators view job sharing as a means of decreasing the number of forced layoffs and as a way of eliminating the need and extra cost of hiring a substitute teacher. Others say job sharing allows them to bring in "new blood," which often adds greater enthusiasm and excitement in the classroom. Included in this article is an outline of key items that administrators expect to see addressed in any proposal for job sharing.

614. Needham, Nancy. "One Job, a Dozen Careers." *NEA Today* 3 (April 1985): 11.

This is an interview with a married couple sharing a sixth-grade teaching position at Weber Elementary School in Arvada, Colorado.

615. Nicholl, Catherine Christie. "Will the Real Professor Please Stand Up?" In *Careers and Couples: An Academic Question*, edited by Leonore Hoffmann and Gloria DeSole. New York: Modern Language Association of America, 1976, pp. 35-36.

Nicholl decides after spending ten years at home with her children to re-enter the teaching profession. Her husband feels he would like to cut back in his teaching load by sharing his job with her. Although approved by the administration, difficulty came in dividing the benefits. Disability insurance was available only to full-time faculty, so the couple decided to accept total compensation under one contract--the man's. This meant that although the wife did half the work, she did not receive a salary in her name.

616. Notowitz, Carol. "Job Sharing for the 80's." *School Library Journal* 28 (February 1982): 33-35.

The pros and cons of job sharing in general are discussed in this article. Also included is a description of the children's librarian position that is shared at a branch of the Public Library of Columbus and Franklin County in Ohio. Bibliography.

617. _____. "A New Way to Work: Job Sharing for Librarians." *School Library Journal* 27 (March 1981): 112.

Two high school librarians (a man and a woman) convince their administration to allow them to job share by using the argument that it would keep two experienced people in the school district. The man works three days a week and the woman works the other two days. She is paid 40 percent of the full-time salary.

618. O'Kane, Patricia K., and Sister Mary Meyer. "Sharing a Faculty Position." *Nursing Outlook* 30 (July/August 1982): 411-413.

Nursing instructors believe job sharing involves using the talents and abilities of two people and viewing the job as a whole, not as fragmented parts. Student feedback to the job sharers was positive although administrative support was not absolute.

619. Oliver, Margurette, Jr. "Job Sharing: Attitudes and Interests among Educational Administration Students." Ph.D. diss., George Peabody College for Teachers of Vanderbilt University, 1990. 231p.

Oliver's dissertation explores job sharing in schools from the perspective of the educational administration student. Those surveyed were graduate students in school administration classes at Western Kentucky University in Bowling Green, Kentucky, and George Peabody College for Teachers of Vanderbilt University in Nashville, Tennessee. Research questions covered the participants' interest in job sharing and their positive and negative attitudes concerning job sharing in addition to identifying relationships between demographics (gender, age, marital status, level of employment, etc.) and answers given by the participants. Tables adequately reflect answers to the research questions. A copy of the survey instrument is included as well as other surveys used in the past. Bibliography.

620. Olmsted, Barney, and Barbara Moorman. "Job Sharing in the Schools: An Administrative View." *Principal's Center Newsletter* (Harvard Graduate School of Education) 3 (Winter 1983): 8-9.

Administrators at several school districts support the concept of job sharing but realize certain questions must be resolved before implementing a job-sharing policy. These include not only matters relating to duties and schedules but also fringe benefits, written policies, and reversibility.

621. *Opening Doors: Encouraging Returners into Teaching as a Career.* London: The National Union of Teachers, 1989. 25p.

The National Union of Teachers suggests job sharing as a means of retaining experienced teachers and attracting others who may have taken a leave of absence to attend to family responsibilities. This booklet identifies how schools, teachers, and pupils can benefit from job sharing. Also included are points for administrators to consider when implementing job-sharing programs.

622. "Pairing Part-Time Teachers—One Veteran and One Tyro—Can Save Money for a School District." *Education Summary* (15 December 1977): 2.

Some administrators view the sharing of an elementary classroom as a way of saving money, especially if one teacher is inexperienced and not earning a very high salary. It would also allow the novice to benefit from the veteran teacher's experiences.

623. "Parkview's Job Sharing Program: The Best of Both Worlds." *Wisconsin School News* 39 (April 1985): 14-15.

Both teachers and administrators in the Parkview, Wisconsin, School District support job sharing in their school. Faculty members enjoy the flexibility and the principal sees job sharing as a way of saving money in addition to meeting the needs of students and teachers. Figures are given for the salary savings.

624. *Part-Time Teachers and How They Work: A Study of Five School Systems.* New York: Catalyst, 1968. 39p. ERIC, ED 028 533.

Reporting on a Catalyst investigation of school districts in five different communities, this study details the partnership teaching program introduced in 1965 in Framingham, Massachusetts, and four other school systems. Reactions of administrators, teachers, and parents are quoted.

625. "Part-Time Work Patterns in Some Melbourne Academic Libraries." *Australian Academic and Research Libraries* 14 (December 1983): 229-234.

Although more academic libraries in Melbourne used permanent part-time staff in 1983 than they did in 1979, job sharing and part-time work have not been totally embraced. Some unions view part-time arrangements as a threat to the interests of full-time employees and management often sees higher administrative costs. Bibliography.

626. "Partnership Teaching: Necessity's Discovery." *Learning* 3 (April 1975): 8+10.

Partnership teaching may be the answer for teachers faced with layoffs due to decreasing enrollments in school districts.

627. Perkins, Stephanie, and Gretchen Davidson Brown. "Job Sharing and the Woman Librarian with Family Responsibilities." *PNLA Quarterly* (Pacific Northwest Library Association) 41 (Summer 1977): 14-17.

Differences between job sharing and part-time employment are explained by these two authors. Also discussed are advantages a library might enjoy if job sharing is instituted. Bibliography.

628. Perlman, Marsha. "When Two Teachers Share One Job." *Graduate Woman* 74 (September/October 1980): 20-21.

Sixth-grade teachers in Longmont, Colorado, share a classroom. At first, the teachers found they were planning too much for a half-day schedule. In addition, their students were playing one teacher against the other, especially when it came time to determine if treats would be allowed at the end of the day. With improved communication and an evaluation of what each teacher's strengths were, the flexible schedules were enjoyed by all.

629. Petchul, Sherry. "Partnership Program Eases Teacher Shortage." *Christian Science Monitor* (New England ed.), 21 October 1967, 2.

In addition to solving teacher shortages, partnership teaching provides for a mix of strengths and talents, as well as a built-in substitute and a fresh teacher entering the classroom at mid-day.

630. Plant, Sheila. "Job Sharing Provides a Useful Alternative." *Canadian Library Journal* 42 (December 1985): 363-367.

Plant defines and describes the advantages of job sharing from both the employers' and employees' perspectives as well as the reluctance encountered from both sides, including union views. Bibliography.

631. Porter, Nona. *Orientation Held for New Members of Partnership Teaching Program.* Boston: Women's Educational and Industrial Union, 1966. 47p. ERIC, ED 012 255.

This document describes the partnership teaching program established in the Boston area and sponsored by the Women's Educational and Industrial Union. After a year, the program had fifty participants. Included here are suggestions for preparing partnership teachers at both the elementary and secondary levels.

632. "Presidential Timbre: The 79th Annual Conference of the California Library Association." *Library Journal* 103 (1 March 1978): 520-523.

At its 1977 annual conference, the California Library Association sponsored a panel discussion on job sharing. Panelists included a teacher, a librarian, and a library director. Discussion involved comments about living on a part-time salary and the kinds of complications faced by administrators and workers.

633. Preston, Mary Ann. "Opinions of Teachers, Students and Parents toward Educational Job Sharing." M.S. thesis, University of Dayton, 1987. 42p.
Preston surveyed teachers, students, and parents to determine their opinions of job sharing. The sample included fifteen job-sharing teachers and twenty-two fifth-grade students in addition to their parents. Copies of all three questionnaires are included as well as quotes (mostly supportive) from teachers and parents who completed the survey. The researcher herself had been sharing teaching duties for five years. Bibliography.

634. Rabinowitz, Nancy, and Peter Rabinowitz. "Some Thoughts on Job Sharing." In *Careers and Couples: An Academic Question*, edited by Leonore Hoffmann and Gloria DeSole. New York: Modern Language Association of America, 1976, pp. 37-41.
These authors enjoy the flexibility of sharing a teaching position. They experience a sense of competition as well as cooperation and have an economic interest in the success of each other because their contract states that if one is fired the college has the option of firing the other as well, or hiring her or him full-time.

635. Rangecroft, Ann. "Job Sharing for Educational Psychologists." *AEP Journal* 2 (Autumn 1983): 18-22.
The author defines job sharing, describes its use in the United Kingdom, and details its use by eight educational psychologists (all women) whom she surveyed in order to get their opinion on the advantages and disadvantages of job sharing. Bibliography.

636. Rapley, Frank E., and Mahlon L. Lantz. "Job Sharing Is Working." *Michigan School Board Journal* 31 (July-August 1984): 21+23-24.
This article recounts the beginnings of job sharing in Kalamazoo, Michigan, from 1979 to 1985 when a total of thirty-five teachers were scheduled for the program. A survey of parents' attitudes toward job sharing was conducted. It was felt

by most that their children had positive reactions to the shared classroom.

637.   "Reduction in Force." *Dialogue: A Review of Labor Management Cooperation in Public Education* 1 (Summer 1984): 1-12. ERIC, ED 259 474.

Job sharing is reported as an alternative for school districts that have suffered a reduction or are facing a possible decrease in their teaching staff. Ways in which job sharing can reduce layoffs are given. Bibliography.

638.   Rees, Lesley, and Vivienne Van Someren. "Personal View." *British Medical Journal* 289 (29 September 1984): 827.

Two pediatric physicians (women) share a position in a teaching hospital. Both wanted to continue their careers and spend time at home with their young children. They feel job sharing requires a "partner who is at the same stage of training, in the same specialty and geographical area, and who is, most importantly, compatible."

639.   Renfroe, Charles. "Job Sharing Is a Popular Option for Teachers, Others." *World of Work Report* 7 (July 1982): 49-51.

According to a survey by New Ways to Work in San Francisco, job sharing is increasing in California school districts. Opportunities for non-certified personnel (teachers' aides, bus drivers, cafeteria workers, and custodians) are also on the rise.

640.   "Report Card on Time Sharing." *Nation's Schools Report* 6 (29 December 1980): 4.

Job sharing can cut costs to school systems by eliminating the need to hire substitute teachers.

641.   Rex, Kathleen. "Two 'Retread' Teachers Find Sharing One Job Suits Their Needs, Allows Time with Families." *Globe and Mail* (Toronto), 4 January 1973, 6.

A Toronto experimental high school—SEED (Shared Experience, Exploration, and Discovery)—offers an alternative to regular secondary school programs and permits a history and a geography teacher to share classroom duties.

642. Reynolds, Anne L., and Catharine King. "Why Not Partnership Librarians?" *Bay State Librarian* 59 (February 1969): 3-4.

Following the example set by partnership teaching programs, partnership librarianship was initiated in the Needham, Massachusetts, Public Library in 1976. Contrasts are made between the teaching program and the sharing of a library position.

643. Rogers, Rick. "Where Part-Time Flexibility Means a Full-Time Bargain." *Guardian* (London), 18 January 1983, 13.

Although teachers' unions feel job sharing can undermine the security of full-time teachers, one couple tries teaching part-time and sharing the tutoring of thirty pupils. Since they do not have overlap time at school, they must consult with each other at home.

644. Rouse, Diane, and Irene Laursen. "Job Sharing in the Wellesley College Science Library: A Preliminary Report." *News Bulletin* (Boston Chapter, Special Libraries Association) 42 (May/June 1976): 49.

The post of assistant to the science librarian is shared by two women—one working on her master's degree and one wishing to spend mornings at home with her children. They have separated their duties while maintaining a familiarity with the other's routines; they communicate via a notebook.

645. Russell, Thyra K. "Job Sharing as Viewed by Illinois Library Directors and Employees." *Library Personnel News* 1 (Fall 1987): 27-28.

Statistics gathered from the author's dissertation on job sharing in Illinois libraries are summarized. The typical library job sharer is described along with attitudes of library directors toward sharing.

646. _____. "Job Sharing in Illinois Libraries." Ph.D. diss., Southern Illinois University at Carbondale, 1987. 154p.

The purpose of this dissertation was to investigate where in Illinois libraries job sharing existed and how these positions were perceived by the job sharers themselves and their library directors. Data revealed 31 out of a total 1,277 libraries had 69 individuals engaged in job sharing. Chapters include a review of the historical development of job sharing (especially in libraries) in addition to the advantages and disadvantages as perceived by both employers and employees. The analysis of the data gleaned from the job sharers' questionnaires includes personal data, employment history, perception of job sharing, characteristics of the job-sharing position, and benefits. The library directors' questionnaires obtained data on their perception of job sharing in general as well as their particular positions. Comparison summaries and conclusions follow. Copies of all questionnaires are included. Bibliography.

647. _____. *Job Sharing: Is It in Your Future?* Paper presented at the Illinois Association of College and Research Libraries (IACRL) Session of the Annual Meeting of the Illinois Library Association, Springfield, IL, 11-13 May 1988. ERIC, ED 307 879.

This paper reports on the author's job-sharing survey of 1,277 libraries in Illinois. Investigation included comments from both the job sharers and their library directors. Advantages, disadvantages, reasons for job sharing, characteristics of the job, and overall effectiveness are identified. Bibliography.

648. Rutledge, Diane B. "Job Permanency: The Academic Librarian's Dilemma Is the Administrator's Challenge for the 1980s." *Journal of Academic Librarianship* 7 (March 1981): 29+41.

Rutledge challenges the innovative library administrator to consider changes in work policies, such as revolving contracts, job sharing, flextime, and part-time professional positions as a means of allowing their library employees to develop professionally. Bibliography.

649. "Sample Job Sharing Policies." *Library Personnel News* 1 (Fall 1987): 28-29.

Job-sharing guidelines from the Akron-Summit County Public Library in Ohio and the Sault Ste. Marie Public Library in Ontario, Canada, are presented here. These are written formal policies that cover such things as application procedures, scheduling, benefits, performance reviews, and resignations or terminations.

650. "Sample Shared Appointment Contracts." In *Careers and Couples: An Academic Question*, edited by Leonore Hoffmann and Gloria DeSole. New York: Modern Language Association of America, 1976, pp. 44-45.

Included here is a sample contract of a shared appointment between a married couple. The terms of the contract are specified for both the husband and wife.

651. Sandler, Rhoda, and Judith Platt. "Job Sharing at Montgomery County." *Library Journal* 98 (1 November 1973): 3234-3235.

Media librarians at Montgomery County Community College in Pennsylvania share the work in the audiovisual services department. In this article, they tell how and why job sharing works for them as well as describing advantages the employer enjoys.

652. Scharffe, William G. "Layoff Is a Dirty Word." *Phi Delta Kappan* 65 (September 1983): 60-61.

School districts should consider job sharing as one alternative to layoffs. The author outlines three elements for successful job-sharing programs--cooperative planning, the opportunity to return to full-time work, and mandatory attendance of all teachers at staff meetings, open houses, and parent conferences.

653. Sciarappa, Kathy. "Two Heads Are Better Than One." *New Hampshire School Boards-Administrators Newsletter* (April 1983): 17-18.

Guidance counselors in the Hollis, New Hampshire, area describe their job-sharing position, which is fully supported by their school principal. Pros and cons of job sharing are included.

654. Scott, Angel. "Equal Shares." *Times Educational Supplement* (London), 2 December 1983, 18.

The author advocates the use of job sharing in the educational system as a means of balancing the teaching staff between men and women, allowing unemployed teachers the opportunity to work, and granting older teachers a means of easing into retirement.

655. Shackelford, Arn. "Job Sharing: The Best of Both Worlds." *Grand Rapids* (MI) *Press*, 28 June 1981, G12.

Two women who are partners in a business also share duties in the continuing education division at Davenport College directing faculty and program development. Also included is a description of social workers in the Grand Rapids school system and probation officers who are sharing responsibilities for half the salary.

656. Shapiro, Eileen C., and Shirley G. Driscoll. "Part-Time Residencies via Shared Scheduling." *Resident & Staff Physician* 24 (December 1978): 66-71.

The authors describe the shared-schedule positions at Harvard Medical School, which are divided by two residents, each working two-thirds to three-quarters time. Each is paid at least half salary and receives the appropriate number of credit hours. In order to provide quality patient care, some overlap time is scheduled for the two residents. Bibliography.

657. "Shared Tenure." *Equal Employment News* (February 1980): 6.

This two-sentence note tells of a husband and wife who share tenure in a full-time teaching position at Earlham College in Richmond, Indiana.

658. "Sharing the Job." *Honolulu Star-Bulletin*, 16 March 1976, B3.

Two neighbors share a college secretarial job in addition to caring for each other's children. (See item No. 705 for a related article.)

659. Shaw, Adrian. "Today's Lesson Is Bringing Up Baby." *Standard* (London), 5 October 1982, 3.

In order to share in raising his son, a physics and social studies teacher divides his teaching duties with his wife. The couple describes the situation as "the best of both worlds" because neither had to give up a job and both could contribute to the care of their child.

660. Shaw, Carole. "One Class, Twice the Teachers." *San Diego* (CA) *Union*, 18 March 1982, North County Panorama [Section] 1+5.

Teachers in Poway, California, Unified School District each work a half day and enjoy teaching the subjects in which they have the strongest interest. Job sharing can cut down on one's personal expenses. For example, wardrobe and child-care expenses can be less for the teacher who works part-time. A drawback from the administrative point-of-view is that part-time teachers receive full fringe benefits, which result in greater costs to the district.

661. Smith, Hal. "Job Sharing." *Blair & Ketchum's Country Journal* 11 (November 1984): 16-17.

Smith identifies his reasons for initiating a job-sharing position at the State University of New York at Binghamton. He shares the writing and editing duties of the faculty/staff newspaper with a woman who previously worked as a freelance writer. They trade work time if necessary but plan only a one-hour overlap on Wednesdays when he comes in to work the last half of the workweek.

662. Smith, Suzanne. "New Law Offers Teachers Opportunity for Job Sharing, Phased Retirement." *World of Work Report* 5 (January 1980): 3-4.

A 1974 California law permits teachers to reduce their schedules from full- to part-time. This, plus encouragement from New Ways to Work (a California-based organization working toward the improvement of part-time work opportunities), has led many school districts to create job-sharing positions for older teachers who wish gradually to phase into retirement. The job-sharing option also became a viable one after Proposition 13 was passed in California in 1978 and many school districts were faced with layoffs.

663. "Some Positive Benefits from Job Sharing." *CABE Journal* (Connecticut Association of Boards of Education) (March 1984): 10.

Cited previously as item No. 507.

664. Sorby, Barbara, and Maureen Pascoe. *Job Sharing: The Great Divide?* Beckett Park [Yorkshire, England]: Leeds Polytechnic, School of Librarianship, 1983. 97p.

This book resulted from a joint project by the authors while enrolled in a course on librarianship at Leeds Polytechnic. They investigated job sharing in the Sheffield city libraries. Questionnaires were used to survey the attitudes of employees and employers in the libraries. Also included are summaries of where job sharing is taking place in other countries and its advantages and disadvantages in addition to basic duties of job-sharing librarians and the views of trade unions in Sheffield. Bibliography.

665. Spencer, Diane. "A Mixture That Can Plug the Gaps." *Times Educational Supplement* (London), 27 January 1989, A5.

This article includes a description of a research project on job sharing conducted by a teacher who had been employed on several fixed-term contracts. The researcher talked with both teachers and administrators to get their opinions of job sharing.

666. *Staffing Alternatives: Use of Retired Persons, Flextime, Job Sharing and Other Suggestions.* Salem, OR: Oregon Department of Education, 1983. 18p. ERIC, ED 243 251.

This booklet outlines three staffing options (early retirement, flextime, and job sharing) for schools in Oregon. Advantages and disadvantages from both viewpoints (sharers and employers) are described as well as a thirteen-point checklist that school districts should review if they are considering implementing job sharing. Bibliography.

667. Stanyon, Mary. "Flexibility: A Threat or a Promise for Women in the Library Profession?" *New Library World* 92 (January 1991): 4-5.

While job sharing allows flexibility in the workplace, the author points out that this flexibility could be seen as a threat, especially to women in the library profession where work is often part-time and pay scales are low. In order for women to benefit from job sharing, there must be "opportunities for promotion, further training, and advancement," just as there would be for anyone employed full-time.

668. *Status Report on the Implementation of Job Sharing in the Department of Education.* Honolulu: Office of the Legislative Auditor, 1979. 14p.

Included in this status report are statistics on the number of teachers who participated in the job-sharing pilot project in Hawaiian schools. The distribution of the job-sharing teachers is identified by district and school, grade level, subject areas, age, ethnic background, and length of service in the Department of Education.

669. Stuchell, John E. "Paired Teaching--Why Not?" *Today's Education* 61 (May 1972): 54.

The author, an elementary school principal, describes a fictitious situation where a newly married couple expecting a child share classroom teaching duties.

670. Sunderland, Helen. "Job Sharing: A New Way to Work." *Librarians for Social Change* 9 (1981): 22-24.

Sunderland says libraries have not readily accepted job-sharing programs because they are not aware of what is involved. She defines job sharing, explains how it works, details the benefits for all involved, and gives the unions' perspective as well as telling prospective sharers how to begin a new job-sharing program.

671. *Tapping Human Resources of the Community for Schools: Applying Partnerships to Teaching.* Storrs, CT: University of Connecticut, School of Education, 1970. 66p. ERIC, ED 043 562.

This document describes a pilot project sponsored by the Hartford College Counseling Center with the purpose of developing partnership teaching and special part-time teaching assignments. Several examples of various ways partners share teaching loads are included as well as an evaluation by all (teachers, principals, colleagues, parents, and children) who participated in the program.

672. "Teachers to Look at Job Sharing." *Chronicle-Herald* (Halifax, Canada), 15 March 1983, 5.

The Nova Scotia Teachers Union approves a resolution calling for the development of job-sharing options for teachers faced with the possibility of layoffs.

673. "Teaching Is Not a Dead-End Street." *Instructor* 89 (February 1980): 106-108+110+112.

Included in this article is a section on partnership teaching, which allows some teachers time off to pursue other professional interests.

674. Teachout, Ann Francee. "Job Sharing and the Role of the Teacher in Elementary Schools." M.A. thesis, San Diego State University, 1982. 83p.

This researcher presents a case study of job sharing in schools. She chose an elementary school district (San Diego County) that employed thirty-two job sharers in sixteen full-time positions. In addition, she surveyed thirty-two full-time teachers and eleven principals. Results describe the job sharers demographically and compare them with the full-time teachers. Both principals and teachers indicated their level of satisfaction with job sharing. Through the use of a Likert scale of measurement, the job sharers indicated their feelings about the partnership operations. Copies of questionnaires and cover letters are included. Bibliography.

675. Terrebonne, Nancy G., and Robert A. Terrebonne. "On Sharing an Academic Appointment." In *Careers and Couples: An Academic Question,* edited by Leonore Hoffmann and Gloria DeSole. New York: Modern Language Association of America, 1976, pp. 30-32.

The authors have experienced negative reactions from prospective employers to proposals for sharing an academic teaching position. The advantages of hiring two for the price of one do not sway administrators who have rules about hiring husbands and wives in the same department.

676. Thomas, Kathleen, Janice McLean, and Patti Delany. "Three into One Does Go! Job Sharing as an Alternative to Full-Time Employment." *Canadian Woman Studies* 6 (Winter 1985): 96-98.

The authors describe how and why the position of co-ordinator of the women's program at Algonquin College in Ottawa came to be split three ways. Each partner works twelve hours a week. In order to share the work and responsibilities equally, they keep two files—a diary and a meeting book. All information needed to communicate effectively is written in one of these books. The development of several work procedures is also included.

677. Tod, Bernadette. "Twice the Expertise, Twice the Experience." *ILEA News* (Inner London Education Authority), 7 May 1987, 6-7.

Tod describes job sharers at elementary schools in the London area. One couple agrees that the advantages outweigh the disadvantages but says it is not always easy. One job-sharing team had to negotiate pay scales for regular hours and overlap time in addition to dealing with a rule that would have prevented them from sharing a senior post.

678. "Trading Places for 11 Years." *Library of Congress Information Bulletin* 50 (15 July 1991): 267.

The position of special events officer at the Library of Congress in Washington, DC, is shared by two women who plan events together through the use of extensive written communication. File folders are kept on all events and every vital detail is written down so that one can pick up where the other left off.

679. Trost, Cathy. "Job Sharing Is Catching On among Teachers Who Want to Work Part-Time." *Wall Street Journal*, 19 March 1985, 1.

School districts and parents support job sharing in this Michigan report.

680. Trown, E. A. "Yesterday's Part-Timers: Tomorrow's Job Sharers?" *Durham and Newcastle Research Review* 10 (Autumn 1983): 95-98.

The Assistant Masters and Mistresses' Association sponsored a survey of variations in part-time teaching opportunities in England and Wales. Teachers who were no longer employed part-time were surveyed. Many indicated a strong interest in part-time work and a desire for increased opportunities in job-sharing programs. Bibliography.

681. Truax, Mary. "Job Sharing: An Alternative to Full-Time Employment." M.A. thesis, California State Polytechnic University, Pomona, 1987. 52p.

This researcher studied job sharing in the public schools in Los Angeles County, California. Questionnaires mailed to the schools' personnel officers were designed to secure data about the schools' use of job sharing and an evaluation of its success. Bibliography.

682. Tugwell, Claudia. "1/2 + 1/2 > 1 Proof: Job Sharing in the Math Classroom." *Manitoba Mathematics Teacher* 11 (March 1983): 43-44.

Reasons for the effectiveness of job-sharing teams are expressed in this article. Hypothetical situations of two teachers sharing one classroom are included.

683. "Two for the Money." *American Education* 14 (August/September 1978): 5.

Teachers at Poolesville Elementary School in Montgomery County, Maryland, divide the teaching day in half. Administrators see an advantage because there is seldom a need to hire a substitute.

684. Unger, Michael. "When a Single Job Is Shared by Two." *Newsday* (Long Island, NY), 22 September 1981, Part II, 4-5.

Presbyterian ministers (husband and wife) share the pastorship of one congregation. While some members of the congregation were hesitant to approve this arrangement, it has proven to be successful. One of the advantages enjoyed by the pastors is the two perspectives they bring to marriage and family counseling sessions.

685. Vincent, Ida. "Academic Library Administrators and Part-Time Work." *Australian Academic and Research Libraries* 10 (September 1979): 150-161.

Vincent surveyed college and university library administrators on their attitudes toward part-time work and their reasons for employing part-time staff. Out of twenty-seven responses, eight examples of job sharing were identified. Tables give statistics on the research and why administrators favored the use of part-time employees. Bibliography.

686. _____. "Womanpower! Part-Time Work and Job Sharing in Libraries." *Australian Library Journal* 27 (December 1978): 330-333.

The Identification of several benefits job sharing offers a library are listed in this article. Also included are problems that may be encountered when part-time employment is introduced in libraries. Bibliography.

687. Vinson, Dotty, and Linda Branam. "Fresh as a Daisy: Job Sharing Offers Chance to Be a Better Teacher and Parent." *Tennessee Teacher* 48 (February 1981): 18-19+30.

The authors describe through a series of questions and answers how job sharing works for them and what makes it a viable work plan for school districts in general.

688. _____. "Job Sharing: They Leave School Fresh as a Daisy." *Tennessee School Boards Bulletin* 32 (July-August 1981): 7-8+16.

Cited above as item No. 687.

689. "Voluntary Part-Time Teaching and Job Sharing Plans." *A Provincial Overview* (Education Relations Commission, Ontario) 5 (January 1984): 2.

Ontario's Education Relations Commission reports that voluntary part-time contracts and job sharing have been offered as a way of reducing the number of layoffs. Results of a survey (1982-83) of 160 collective bargaining agreements showed fifteen schools offered part-time contracts and ten schools offered job sharing. The names of the schools are listed in this article.

690.   "Voluntary Part-Time Teaching and Job Sharing Plans."
       Canadian School Executive 4 (November 1984): 33.
       A condensation of item No. 689.

691.   Wade, Maureen. "Job Sharing in a Public Library." *Librarians
       for Social Change* 9 (1981): 27.
       Two Camden, England, librarians in charge of buying
       books for three large reference libraries divide their duties and
       split the workweek. While one woman takes a maternity leave,
       her partner switches to full-time work.

692.   Wallace, Joan. "Job Sharing: The New Way to Work Part-
       Time." *Chatelaine* 57 (March 1984): 52+104-105.
       School teachers in the Vancouver area are showing other
       Canadians that job sharing can be a viable alternative to full-time
       employment. This article describes the first (1983) national
       survey of job sharers in Canada and outlines four steps to
       establishing a job-sharing position.

693.   Waters, Paula N., and Sharon Y. Nickols. "Management of
       Family and Employment Roles: Does Job Sharing Help?" In
       Families and Work, edited by Beulah M. Hirschlein and William
       J. Braun. Stillwater, OK: Oklahoma State University, 1982, pp.
       125-132. ERIC, ED 247 446.
       This article describes a survey of job sharers and full-time
       employees in two universities in Oklahoma and a public school
       system in Kansas. Workers' perceptions regarding their
       employment and family responsibilities, time flexibility, and job
       satisfaction are compared. Bibliography.

694.   Waters, Paula Nadine. "A Comparative Study of Job Sharing
       and Full-Time Employees: Job Satisfactions and Management of
       Family Roles." M.S. thesis, Oklahoma State University, 1982.
       96p.
       Waters surveyed full-time and job-sharing employees
       (secretaries and teachers) in three educational institutions:
       Oklahoma State University, Panhandle State University, and the
       Wichita Public School System. Her purpose was "to compare
       employee perceptions of job sharing and full-time employment
       and to examine the effects of each type of schedule on the lives

of employees." Specifically, she compared employee perceptions in the following areas: benefit programs, job satisfaction, and attitudes toward employment and family roles in addition to time flexibility. Bibliography.

695. Waugh, Audrey. "How to Have Your Cake and Eat It Too [, the Trend] to Half-Time Partner Teaching." *Prime Areas* (Journal of the British Columbia Primary Teachers' Association) 21 (Spring 1979): 47-48.

This article is "addressed to" teachers interested in half-time work. Waugh details how she and her elementary teaching partner divide the teaching, supervision, and record-keeping duties of one classroom. In addition to switching at noon on a daily basis, at mid-year they switch time blocks—the morning teacher to afternoon and vice-versa.

696. Weil, Marsha. "Oversupply as Opportunity: An Exploration of Job Sharing and Inservice Education." In *Creative Authority and Collaboration: A Collection of Position Papers.* Syracuse, NY: Syracuse University, National Dissemination Center, 1977, pp. 103-114.

Weil defines job sharing, identifies some case studies that have been reported, and looks at job sharing as a way of facilitating inservice education. She concludes that job sharing allows flexibility in a teaching job, which, in turn, permits more time and energy for inservice education, including advanced training in the form of sabbaticals, apprenticeships, or teacher-training programs.

697. Wilce, Hilary. "ILEA Throws Open 30 Jobs in Pilot Sharing Scheme." *Times Educational Supplement* (London), 11 May 1984, 15.

The Inner London Education Authority (ILEA) announces the availability of job sharing for primary and secondary teachers despite a disagreement with representatives from the Inner London Teachers' Association over additional money for paid overlap time.

698. _____. "Job Sharing Gets a Pilot Scheme in London." *Times Educational Supplement* (London), 2 December 1983, 5.

Teachers in London are reviewing a proposal from the Inner London Education Authority (ILEA) on the establishment of job-sharing programs. The problem of greatest concern expressed by teachers is payment for overlap time.

699. _____. "London Classrooms Set for Job Share." *Times Educational Supplement* (London), 4 April 1986, 1.

The Inner London Education Authority (ILEA) approves job sharing for virtually all its classrooms. ILEA also supports the idea "that sharers must be given consultation time."

700. _____. "Profiting from Shares." *Times Educational Supplement* (London), 13 April 1984, 13.

Wilce reports on a study by Margaret Angier (see item No. 499) on job sharing in ten Sheffield schools where the operation ran smoothly. Reasons are identified as well as how teaching duties were divided.

701. Wilcox, Helen. "Calling All Job Sharers." *AUT Woman* (Association of University Teachers, London) 16 (Spring 1989): unnumbered.

London's Association of University Teachers supports job-sharing arrangements because of the freedom it gives an individual to pursue other interests. Job sharers each contribute to form a partnership that proves beneficial to a teaching department. A weakness of the arrangement is that each employee may be expected to do a full-time job while receiving only half the salary.

702. Williams, Charles Richard. "An Analysis of Job Sharing by Teachers." Ed.D. diss., University of Southern California, 1989. 121p.

In his dissertation, Williams studies job sharing by teachers in California public schools. He surveys a six-county area--three in northern California and three in the southern part of the state. The perceptions of both the teachers and their principals as to the satisfaction, benefits, and disadvantages as well as acceptance of job sharing are investigated and analyzed via tables. Demographic characteristics of the teachers are included in addition to copies of all questionnaires and letters. Bibliography.

703. Winkler, Karen J. "Two Who Share One Academic Job Say the Pro's Outnumber the Con's." *Chronicle of Higher Education* 19 (3 December 1979): 3-4.

A married couple shares an American history teaching position at Scripps College in California. They each have tenure, faculty voting privileges, an office, and are eligible for sabbatical leaves and travel money.

704. "Women in CIPFA: Returning to Work." *Public Finance and Accountancy* (31 May 1991): 8-10.

In this article, four women who are members of the Chartered Institute of Public Finance and Accountancy (CIPFA) report on various ways they have returned to work after a break in their careers. Jane Smith, an instructor at Wolverhampton Business School, returned by sharing a teaching position. She and her partner split the position forty/sixty. Smith reports that it has been an "ideal compromise between family and career."

705. "Women Share Paycheck, Children." *Christian Science Monitor* (Midwestern ed.), 5 April 1976, 12.

Neighbors share a secretarial job at Chatham College in Pittsburgh, Pennsylvania, and child-care duties at home. Each woman works three days one week and two days the next week. (See item No. 658 for a related article.)

706. "Work Sharing." In *Managing the One-Person Library*, by Guy St. Clair and Joan Williamson. London: Butterworths, 1986, pp. 92-96.

Although entitled "work sharing," these pages define and describe job sharing and show how it can be used to manage a one-person library such as a small public, corporate, or association library. Advantages and disadvantages are listed.

Government

707. Aikin, Olga. "Exclusion from Job Sharing." *Personnel Management* 21 (November 1989): 71-72.

A branch librarian sued the Wandsworth (London) Borough Council alleging discrimination because she was not allowed to job share. The council had a policy excluding management positions from job sharing; the policy was upheld by the courts.

708. Alison, Michael. "Job Sharing in Practice." *Management Review & Digest* 10 (April 1983): 8-10.

The British government provides grants to employers who willingly split full-time jobs in order to hire the unemployed, including youth who leave school early and those who want only part-time work because of age, family, or social commitments.

709. Alpert, Helen. "Flexitime, Flexiwork, Flexijobs & Retiree Job Sharing." *Retirement Living* 17 (May 1977): 23-25.

Pairing, sharing, and splitting are all ways of dividing a full-time job in which retirees have shown an interest. Flexible working hours and job sharing are also becoming popular in Western Europe.

710. Andresen, Karen, and Barbara Jason-White. "How Job Sharing Works in Novato." *Western City* 65 (August 1989): 8-11.

Recruiting for the job-sharing position of administrative assistant for the city of Novato in northern California yielded a number of highly qualified and talented people. The authors describe how their job evolved and tell of the benefits they enjoy as well as the advantages to their employer.

711.   Buck, Claudia. "Job Sharing No Longer a Quixotic Notion." *San Francisco Examiner*, 30 December 1985, B1+B6.

Buck reports that job sharing has become more acceptable in California state government than when it was proposed in 1979 by two women who wanted to share the Employment Development Department's lobbyist position. She reports on other state government positions that are being shared and why this work alternative is attractive to certain people.

712.   Burningham, Sally. "Two Brains Are Better Than One." *Health Service Journal* 97 (5 February 1987): 160.

The position of general manager of community health services for the Camberwell, England, health authority was assigned to two women who were interviewed jointly and were able to offer a wide range of skills between them. The sharers believe that total joint responsibility for a job means joint determination of management policies.

713.   "Careers Staff Appeal over Job Share Ban." *Scotsman* (Edinburgh), 10 January 1986, 9.

Women employed by the Strathclyde, Scotland, Regional Council appeal a decision forbidding them to share a job and claim the council is guilty of sex discrimination. (See item No. 722 for a related article.)

714.   Carter, Don. "They 'Packaged' Themselves for Career." *Seattle Post-Intelligencer*, 15 January 1978, F2+F3.

An urban planning team in Puget Sound, Washington, enjoys the personal benefits of sharing. Although it may require more time communicating, the supervisors think the benefits to the city outweigh the disadvantages.

715.   _____. "They Wanted to Unlock 'Golden Handcuffs'." *Seattle Post-Intelligencer*, 15 January 1978, F2.

Psychologists at a veterans' hospital in the State of Washington share the responsibility for thirty-five patients. While the assessment of patients' problems, group counseling, and progress evaluations are shared, individual counseling sessions are not. Both doctors feel the patients and the hospital benefit from the shared arrangement.

716. Causey, Mike. "Job Sharing Test Sought." *Washington Post*, 21 May 1989, D2.

Causey reports on a bill called the "Federal Flexible Work Arrangements Act" that was introduced in Congress. This legislation would allow individuals working for the federal government to share a single job. After eighteen months, agencies would be required to report to Congress on the success or failure of the job-sharing plan.

717. _____. "A Test for Job Sharing." *Washington Post*, 7 November 1990, C2.

Causey reports that federal employees who wish to reduce their full-time work load will be able to participate in job-sharing programs to be tested in Boston, Chicago, Los Angeles, and Washington, DC.

718. Chandler, Frances J., and James A. Johnson. "Attitudes toward Job Sharing: A Case Study of the Employment and Immigration Commission." *Canadian Public Administration* 32 (Winter 1989): 633-640.

The authors surveyed in June 1987 both full-time employees and job sharers at the Employment and Immigration Commission in Ontario. After providing demographic information, sharers were asked to specify reasons for their job sharing. Results are reported in this article along with comparisons between full-time employees and job sharers. Comparison is also made between this study and other Canadian research studies that have investigated workers' attitudes toward job sharing.

719. Cirilli, Mary, Diane Jones, and Kathryn Moore. "Job Sharing in Wisconsin." *Intergovernmental Personnel Notes* (January-February 1980): 13-15.

Project JOIN (Job Options and Innovations) began in Wisconsin in 1976 with the objective of increasing the job satisfaction and productivity of its state employees. This article identifies four project goals and describes recruitment procedures, job development, and research findings.

720. Coates, Anne. "A Day in the Life of Cheryl Blake." *Parents* (British ed.) (November 1984): 112.

A British mother describes her typical job-sharing day. She and her partner try to divide non-urgent work and deal with urgent problems as they arise. The two women also employ the same babysitter for their children.

721. Cook, Lindsay. "Two for the Price of One." *Guardian* (London), 4 August 1984, 19.

British mothers and fathers both rejoiced when the courts found in favor of a single parent's request to share her job. Training sessions on the procedures and advantages of job sharing have been organized by a London-based firm promoting alternative staffing, New Ways to Work.

722. Cunningham, Jennifer. "Women Win Right to Share a Post." *Glasgow* (Scotland) *Herald*, 31 January 1986, 1.

A Scottish court rules in favor of two women employees of the Strathclyde Regional Council who had appealed the council's ban on job sharing. The council was told to change the terms and conditions of employment for the two women and to establish a policy allowing job sharing for other employees. (See item No. 713 for a related article.)

723. Curran, Nancy. "Professional Worker/Committed Parent." *Swarthmore College Bulletin* 85 (February 1988): 11-14.

Co-workers in the Department of Planning and Growth Management for the city of Austin, Texas, opt for an alternative to the traditional nine-to-five working schedule. In order to have more time for their children, they share the position but stress the need for good communication so that either partner can handle business calls.

724. Eaker, Kathryn. "Job Sharing--A Growing Alternative to the 40-Hour Grind." *Sacramento Bee*, 13 July 1980, D1+D3.

Job sharing is seen by many to be the answer for workers who want to cut back on their work time. This article looks at three couples--two in government and one in private business--who share jobs. Also included is another author's view of the limited applications of job sharing and why she believes it will always be a women's issue.

725. Eskes, Dave. "Share the Work . . . and the Wealth." *Phoenix Gazette*, 27 May 1981, D1+D3.

Social workers see the advantages of sharing caseloads, which allows them leisure time to pursue other interests such as more education.

726. Euers, Myra. "The Double Act That Could Top the Jobs Bill." *Public Service* (National and Local Government Officers Association, London) (April 1984): 10-11.

Euers reports on how job sharing differs from job splitting and talks with sharers at the Camden and Bristol branches of the National and Local Government Officers Association (NALGO). The latter describe their workday in addition to the pluses they enjoy because of job sharing.

727. *Evaluation of Job Sharing for Nurses in the Department of Health: Final Report.* Honolulu: Office of the Legislative Auditor, 1989. 18p.

After Hawaii's legislature introduced job sharing in the public sector, it established a similar program for nurses in its Department of Health. This booklet records the findings and recommendations' on job sharing subsequent to the nurses' two-year pilot project. Included among the findings are long-term considerations and flexibility in setting work hours for nurses.

728. "Fighting to Keep Equal Opportunities Alive." *Labour Research* 77 (February 1988): 9-12.

Job sharing is a way of providing equal opportunities for women workers. Many of the local government authorities in England have job-sharing policies in effect.

729. *Final Report on Shared Positions (Expanded Use of Part-Time Employment).* Sacramento: California State Personnel Board, Policy and Standards Division, 1978. 58p.

This document reports on the shared positions project which took place in various governmental offices in the State of California from September 1976 to March 1977. Included are summaries of both the supervisors' and participants' evaluations of productivity, quality of work, job satisfaction, and other items such as administrative costs and benefits paid to employees. Sample report forms as well as copies of the evaluation forms and supervisors' questionnaires are included along with a listing of job classifications that were shared. Bibliography.

730. *First Status Report on Job Sharing in Hawaii State Government: A Report to the Governor and the Legislature of the State of Hawaii.* Honolulu: Office of the Legislative Auditor, 1991. 16p.

Hawaii's state legislature first established job sharing in 1978 in the Department of Education. This project continued for six years. The second project began in 1982 in the public library system and ran for four years. A third project for nurses in the Department of Health began in FY 1986-87 and lasted until FY 1989-90. All of these work arrangements were found to be cost-effective, desirable, and feasible. Hence, the legislature has extended job-sharing opportunities throughout state government--to the executive branch, the University of Hawaii, the judiciary, the Legislative Reference Bureau, the Office of the Auditor, and the Office of the Ombudsman--to begin FY 1990-91 and continue through FY 1993-94.

731. Gaze, Harriet. "It Takes Two." *Nursing Times: NT* 85 (25 October 1989): 19.

Gaze details what job sharing can mean for nurses working in the United Kingdom's National Health Service (NHS). She also briefly describes an Institute of Manpower Studies report that investigated job sharing in the NHS.

732. Gibb, Frances. "Women's Employment 'Strengthened' by Tribunal Job Share Rule." *Times* (London), 27 October 1986, 3.

A Glasgow court has agreed that a woman employee of the Greater Glasgow Health Board was discriminated against when she was not allowed to share her job after her maternity leave. (See item No. 741 for a related article.)

733. "Grants to Encourage Sharing of Jobs." *Times* (London), 28 July 1982, 1.

In an effort to offer part-time work to people receiving unemployment benefits, the British government has announced plans for a job-splitting scheme.

734. Green, Valerie. "Half a Job Is Better Than None!" *Oxford* (England) *Mail*, 3 July 1986, 8.

Two British probation officers encourage others interested in job sharing to ask their employers about it. The flexible work arrangement of the probation officers provides them both with the right mix of work and family.

735. Griffiths, Prue. "Changing Patterns of Work." *Industrial Society* 65 (September 1983): 6-7.

Griffiths identifies both good and bad points of the British government's job-splitting scheme. While this scheme should provide the unemployed with jobs, there is also the danger that employees who want full-time work might be compelled to reduce their working hours.

736. Hamilton, Mildred. "A Couple Pioneers in Job Sharing." *San Francisco Examiner and Chronicle*, 25 April 1976, Sunday Scene [Section] 3.

Employment and child-rearing duties are shared by a San Francisco couple working as the regional director of a community service agency. They split responsibilities for job corps programs in a four-state territory. Other government positions are also being shared in the San Francisco Bay area.

737. Harper, Keith. "CBI Tells How to Avoid Claims by Job Sharers." *Guardian* (London), 6 October 1982, 3.

The British government's job-splitting plan could result in workers claiming full-time employment rights and/or unfair dismissals.

738. _____. "Job Splitting in Doubt as Firms Ignore Scheme." *Guardian* (London), 19 July 1983, 3.

In an effort to continue the job-splitting scheme and encourage more employer participation, British labor officials announced changes designed to give employers greater flexibility.

739. _____. "New Cash for Firms If Jobs Are Split." *Guardian* (London), 28 July 1982, 1+24.

   The job-splitting scheme announced by the British government provides a monetary grant for employers instituting job-splitting positions that result in the recruitment of unemployed workers. The scheme is designed to attract married women with children and employees approaching retirement.

740. Haskin, David. "Job Sharing Debut Watched Closely." *Milwaukee Journal*, 3 November 1976, Accent [Section] 3.

   Haskin identifies two women who are the first to share their state job (assistant telecommunications director) under a federally sponsored project to develop, test, and evaluate the cost and productivity of sharing jobs in the Wisconsin civil service system.

741. "Health Visitor Wins Sex Bias Case." *Scotsman* (Edinburgh), 12 August 1986, 8.

   The Greater Glasgow Health Board is successfully sued by an employee who was not granted a job-sharing position. Government officials see this as a major step forward for women workers who wish to continue their careers in addition to child-care responsibilities. (See item No. 732 for a related article.)

742. Hetherington, Barbara, and Mike Everley. "Shared Responsibility." *Industrial Society* 67 (September 1985): 24-25+42.

   An office of the Paddington, England, Churches Housing Association employs a job-sharing team and the manager outlines the advantages and disadvantages both to employers and employees.

743. Howie, Caroline. "When Two into One Can Work Like Magic." *Independent* (England), 6 April 1987, 12.

   Frustrated by the lack of free personal time, two women employees of the British National Health Service decide to share a position. They are paid for an eighteen-hour week but each agreed to work twenty-one hours to include overlap time for communication with one another.

744. Hyndman, Connie, and Janelle Personius. "Job Sharing in the Head Nurse Role–Decreased Stress." *Nursing Administration Quarterly* 7 (Winter 1983): 35-41.

   Head nurses at the Veterans Administration Medical Center located in American Lake, Washington, decide to try sharing a position in order to reduce stress and burnout. Included in this article is the outline of possible problems and solutions that they presented to hospital administrators. Their proposed time schedule included one week on, one week off. Bibliography.

745. Jacob, Louise. "U.K.'s Job Splitting Scheme Takes Heat from Unions and Work Groups." *Work Times* 1 (Winter 1983): 5-6.

   Jacob explains why the experiment with job splitting in the United Kingdom will not accomplish its intention, which is to alleviate unemployment. She believes the plan will encourage low pay and that job splitters will not be protected from unfair dismissal. The differences between job sharing and job splitting are noted.

746. Jacobson, Sandra A. *Job Sharing as a Management Tool: A Feasibility Study of the Concept of Job Sharing for Hawaii State Civil Service System Employees.* Honolulu: Department of Personnel Services, 1979. 175p.

   This study not only analyzes the question of whether job sharing should be introduced but also how it can be incorporated into the State of Hawaii's Civil Service System. Included in this detailed study is an overview of job sharing, state legislative history of part-time employment and interest in job sharing, union concerns, fringe benefits, program development, initiation, and a pilot project as well as cost analyses. Appendices include a supervisory survey report and a program monitoring form. Bibliography.

747. "Job Share Scheme to Be Widened in Scope." *Times* (London), 16 March 1985, 3.

   The British government has increased the amount of money offered to employers who take advantage of the job-splitting scheme by dividing a full-time position into two part-time jobs.

748. "A Job Shared." *Camden Magazine* (London Borough of Camden) (August 1986): 16.

Local government politicians (both women) for the London Borough of Camden share their councilor position. One would rather attend meetings in the daytime and she concentrates on London-wide issues while the other attends evening meetings and works with Camden-related items.

749. *Job Sharing and National Insurance Costs for 1988-1989.* London: New Ways to Work, 1988. 4p.

Charts showing how much national insurance British employers must pay per week for full-time employees versus job sharers are given in these fact sheets.

750. "Job Sharing Being Tried in U.S.--Wisconsin Experiment." *Ironwood* (MI) *Daily Globe*, 30 March 1976, 6.

A Wisconsin job-sharing test of at least twenty-five existing state jobs is funded through a grant from the U.S. Department of Labor. A study of the experiment will be conducted over a two-year period to determine the effects of having two people share one job.

751. "Job Sharing Concept Worth Serious Examination." *Milwaukee Journal*, 18 March 1976, 1.

This editorial supports a two-year project that will test the feasibility of job sharing in Wisconsin.

752. "Job Sharing: DOA's Involved in the Wave of the Future." *DOA Today* (Wisconsin Department of Administration) (November 1976): 1+4.

Wisconsin's Department of Administration is allowing job sharing and flexible-hour workdays by taking part in Project JOIN (Job Options and Innovations). Definitions of pairing, sharing, and splitting are included in this article.

753. *Job Sharing for Federal Employees.* Washington, DC: U.S. Office of Personnel Management, 1990. 20p.

This U.S. document contains precise, detailed answers to many questions concerning job sharing. Pages cover the following topics: reasons for job sharing, jobs suitable for sharing, advising employees, finding a partner, restructuring a position, scheduling, performance evaluations, and merit promotions. Also included are several scheduling options, tips for better communication, and hints for supervisors.

754. "Job Sharing Gains in Popularity." *DOA Today* (Wisconsin Department of Administration) (February 1978): 4.

Nine employees of Wisconsin's Department of Administration are participating in job sharing. One worker reports that even though she is receiving a lower salary, she is not spending as much for "child care, fast food, and clothes for work."

755. *Job Sharing Guide*. Helena: State of Montana, Department of Administration, Personnel Division, 1984. 37p.

The Montana Legislature formally approved in 1983 the establishment of job sharing for its governmental agencies and employees. This guide is "designed to provide assistance to state supervisors, managers, and employees in administering job-sharing arrangements." It includes information on evaluating positions for job sharing, work planning, performance appraisal, making the proposal, managing the arrangement, replacing a partner, and benefits. The guide includes a copy of the employee appraisal form.

756. *Job Sharing in the Health Service*. London: New Ways to Work, 1989. 8p.

The United Kingdom's National Health Service encourages more part-time employment, including job sharing, which can promote equal opportunities, help solve skilled staff shortages, and make recruitment easier. This booklet includes examples of nurses, physicians, and other health professionals who are job sharing.

757. *Job Sharing in the Public Sector*. San Francisco: New Ways to Work, 1979. 79p. ERIC, ED 197 089.

This book details several factors that affect the successful designing and implementing of job-sharing programs in addition to proposing a model program. It continues with six case histories of job-sharing pilot projects in state, county, and local government agencies in Massachusetts, Wisconsin, and California (Santa Clara County, Santa Cruz County, the city of Palo Alto, and the State of California). Bibliography.

758. "Job Sharing Leads to Better Quality Work, Greater Satisfaction." *Campus Report* (Stanford University), 15 October 1975, 7.

This article reports on a case study undertaken by Stanford University students in a political science class. The study detailed three shared positions (animal control officer, naturalist, and librarian) in the Palo Alto city government and was facilitated by the Action Research Liaison Office at Stanford University. (See item No. 824 for a copy of the case study.)

759. "Job Sharing Plan a 3-Year Success for City Manager." *World of Work Report* 2 (May 1977): 57.

In Palo Alto, California, two people have successfully directed the city's organizational research and development office for three years.

760. "Job Sharing Project Described by Writers." *Capital Times* (Madison, WI), 28 June 1977, 34.

Project JOIN (Job Options and Innovations) investigators Carol Lobes, Diane Lindner Jones, and Mary Cirilli explain the purpose of the project and why it is important to Wisconsin city and state employees.

761. *Job Sharing: Putting Policy into Practice: The Local Authority Experience.* London: New Ways to Work, 1987. 77p.

This major study represents the findings of a survey conducted by the Equal Opportunities Commission in 1986 of local governmental authorities throughout the United Kingdom. Chapters include summaries of the analysis of questionnaires, a copy of the questionnaire, the practical details (how policies were developed, issues that were considered, and how the job-sharing scheme was put into practice). Seven detailed case studies are included.

762. *Job Sharing Report, July 1, 1980-December 31, 1981.* St. Paul, MN: Department of Employee Relations, 1981. 44p.

This document reports on eighteen months of Minnesota's job-sharing program, which provided for fifty full-time classified positions within ten agencies to be shared. Included are chapters on supervisory/administrative time, direct/indirect job-sharing costs and savings, and job-sharing performance in addition to indications of job-sharer satisfaction/dissatisfaction. Copies of questionnaires sent to prospective job sharers, supervisors, and personnel officers as well as the sharers themselves after six months are also part of this report.

763. "Job Sharing Test Funded." *Milwaukee Journal*, 2 April 1976, Accent [Section] 13.
Cited previously as item No. 750.

764. *Job Splitting Scheme*. London: Department of Employment, 1985. 11p.
Written to answer questions about the job-splitting scheme open to all employers in Great Britain, this booklet answers the following questions: How does it work? Under what conditions do jobs qualify? Who can fill these jobs? How is payment of the job-splitting grant made? How does the scheme affect the benefits of those employed under the grant?

765. *The Job Splitting Scheme: Response of the Equal Opportunities Commission to the Department of Employment*. Manchester, England: Equal Opportunities Commission, 1983. 12p.
The Equal Opportunities Commission is interested in promoting equal employment opportunities for women. Job sharing is one way to accomplish this goal. A comparison between job splitting and job sharing is undertaken in this booklet. Points are made in favor of job sharing over job splitting, which may not offer equal employment opportunities.

766. *Job Splitting Scheme: What You Should Know About Working in a Split Job*. London: Department of Employment, 1982. 5p.
This pamphlet defines an individual's part-time employment rights and benefits and describes how the job-splitting scheme will affect those rights.

767. Kailer, Pat. "50/50 Job Sharing in Los Alamos." *Albuquerque* (NM) *Journal*, 24 September 1978, C1+C2.

Two energy information specialists share one position at New Mexico's Los Alamos Scientific Laboratory. Both women had been working part-time in different divisions but decided to work together in the public information office. With an hour overlap in their schedules, they enjoy brainstorming on a daily basis. Sidebar indicates job-sharing programs are increasing.

768. Kennedy, Jeanne L., Charles W. Gossett, Christine M. Sierra, Cheryl A. Stewart, and Jay Rounds. "Job Sharing--A Look at Palo Alto's Program." *Western City* (Official League Magazine of the West) 52 (August 1976): 12-13.

This article is based on an unpublished study conducted by Stanford University students on job sharing in municipal government in the city of Palo Alto, California. (See item No. 824.) Detailed here are the differences between part-time and job sharing. Also included are the benefits (flexible scheduling, productivity, and continuity) of job sharing to the city and how a program can be implemented.

769. Kilborn, Peter T. "Milwaukee Helps Pace U.S. as Innovator for Workplace." *New York Times*, 12 October 1989, 1+11.

The Milwaukee city government is a supporter of alternative work schedules by allowing flextime, four-day workweeks, and job sharing. The supervisor of a job-sharing team in the city treasurer's office says he prefers job sharers to full-time employees. It is also supported by the local unions in the city.

770. Kleiman, Carol. "2 Share Job as Governor's Aide." *Chicago Tribune*, 27 December 1981, Section 15, 1.

The position of office manager for the governor of Illinois' Chicago office is shared by two employees (a man and a woman). One works three days a week while the other works two. The salary is prorated along with benefits: each receives half the vacation, personal, and sick leave time provided a full-time employee.

771. Knickerbocker, Brad. "Government Moves to Hire More Part-Time Employees." *Christian Science Monitor*, 8 March 1978, 6.

Legislation has been passed in several states to establish specific programs or policies designed to increase the number of part-time employees. This includes implementing shared jobs that officials in various state government positions have used to their advantage.

772. Lane, Millicent. "Job Sharers Blaze Path Here." *Lansing* (MI) *State Journal*, 12 May 1981, B5.

Ingham County, Michigan, employees began job sharing as part of a federally funded project. Included are positions in the health department and probate court.

773. Leadbeater, Charles. "Part-Time Jobs Initiative to Be Launched Today." *Financial Times* (London), 6 April 1987, 8.

A job-sharing plan is announced by the British government to replace the "job-splitting scheme" that was previously in effect. The hope is that companies will increase part-time jobs for workers other than married women who have been employed in most of the earlier positions. Employers are encouraged to fill the part-time positions with people receiving unemployment benefits.

774. *The Legal Context to Job Sharing.* London: New Ways to Work, 1989. 4p.

This fact sheet details how the law affects job sharing in England. It describes several court cases involving legal rights to job share.

775. Leslie, Jane. "Job Sharing Helps Solve Employment Dilemma." *Citizen* (Ottawa), 20 May 1980, 70.

Counselors at the Canada Employment Centre who share one position believe their employer benefited by not losing two valuable employees. There can, however, be problems with promotions, attitudes of co-workers, and being prevented (as part-time workers) from paying into retirement plans.

776. Lloyd, John. "Schemes to Cut Jobless." *Financial Times* (London), 28 July 1982, 1+30.

A job-splitting scheme is introduced by the British government. It will pay grants to companies that employ two part-time workers instead of one full-time worker. The plan encourages employers to provide part-time work for people who have been unemployed for twelve months or more.

777. Long, Marion C., and Susan W. Post. "Alternative Work Schedules: The State and Local Experience." *Intergovernmental Personnel Notes* (January-February 1980): 9-12+16.

One type of alternative staffing implemented by several state governments is job sharing. This article mentions programs established in California, Colorado, Hawaii, Maryland, Massachusetts, and Wisconsin that are characteristic of how job sharing has increased the number of part-time employees. Bibliography.

778. Lovelace, Judith. "Long Hours, Ill Health–All Part of the Job." *Local Government Chronicle* (London), 12 June 1987, 18.

Women chief executives who also have families are often under a great deal of pressure at work and at home. Part-time employment via job sharing is being offered as an alternative to the pressures of full-time work and family needs.

779. Martin, Brendan. "Partners in Time." *Social Work Today* 22 (10 January 1991): 13-15.

Social work "team leaders" identify the reasons they have successfully shared one position. Instead of sharing supervision of the total team, they are each responsible for half of it but are on call in emergencies for the other half. They discuss differences of opinion before meetings so they do not disagree in public. A sidebar describes social workers who job share at the liver transplant unit at the Queen Elizabeth Hospital in Birmingham, England.

780. Meager, Nigel, James Buchan, and Charlotte Rees. *Job Sharing in the National Health Service*. Brighton, England: Institute of Manpower Studies, 1989. 161p.

This report presents data on the first survey of job sharing in the United Kingdom's National Health Service (NHS). The study includes detailed chapters on the rationale for job sharing, its advantages and disadvantages, employment costs, and the organization and management of job sharing in addition to specifics on what jobs are being shared in the NHS. Included also is a copy of the questionnaire that was distributed to the health authorities and boards.

781. Miller, Joe. "Whatever Happened to Job Splitting?" *Initiatives* 2 (February 1985): 3-5.

Miller details the British job-splitting scheme announced in July 1982. In addition to describing the differences between job sharing and job splitting, he lists employees' rights and explains why the job-splitting plan has not worked.

782. "New Job Split Scheme under Fire--'Bars Women and Devalues Job Sharing'." *Personnel Management* 15 (February 1983): 11.

This article argues that the British government's job-splitting scheme discriminates against women who are not claiming unemployment benefits and who only want part-time work. It warns against confusing job splitting with job sharing.

783. "New Job Splitting Grant to be £750." *Employment Gazette* 90 (October 1982): 413.

Detailed in this article are points about who can fill a job that has been split, under what conditions, and how the government grant will be paid.

784. Nishimura, Charles H., Lloyd K. Migita, and Stanley K. Okinaka. *The Feasibility of Job Sharing by Public Employees in Hawaii: Some Preliminary Considerations.* Honolulu: Legislative Reference Bureau, State of Hawaii, 1977. 133p. ERIC, ED 158 016.

This publication presents an overview of job sharing, looks at arguments for and against, gives hypothetical job-sharing models, and identifies cost factors concerning job sharing and unemployment insurance in order to determine the feasibility of implementing job sharing in state and county governments. Included are tables listing the annual employee benefit costs with comparisons for several hypothetical jobs. Bibliography.

785. "On the Job: A Day or Two in the Life of Job Sharer Corinne Sweet." *Company* (London), (June 1988): 124-125.

Women senior managers in a London local government's personnel department share the job of improving conditions for women council employees. Shared duties include these: training people, investigating complaints of sexual harassment, promoting policy, attending interviews, and negotiating with unions.

786. *Part-Time and Job Sharing: Issues for New York State.* Albany, NY: Part-Time/Shared Job Project, NYS Department of Civil Service [1985]. 78p.

This book contains presentations and discussions from a conference held in Albany on September 18, 1984. Included is a speech by Linda Glick entitled "A Guide to Job Sharing" with a section on "Choosing Your Partner." Also included is a chapter on case studies in job sharing with discussion from a supervisor's (male) viewpoint and that of two women who share a position under his direction in the New York State Department of Health.

787. *Part-Time Careers in Portland.* Portland, OR: American Association of University Women, 1978. 164p.

Job sharing is mentioned briefly in this discussion of part-time careers. Included in Appendix II is a summary of job-sharing legislation (for state employees) that was passed in Oregon.

788. *Part-Time Schedules: A Guide for NYS Supervisors and Managers.* Albany, NY: Part-time/Shared Job Project, NYS Department of Civil Service, 1985. 47p.

This handbook was prepared to provide guidance for New York State agencies and employees utilizing part-time schedules. As a form of part-time employment, job sharing was included. Examples of problems and possible solutions along with ways for sharers to improve their performance are summarized.

789. "Permanent Part-Time City Jobs." *San Francisco Examiner*, 12 February 1976, 24.

San Francisco's city government officials are encouraged by both men and women to allow job sharing in local government positions.

790. Phillips, Angela. "Hard Luck, Mum." *Independent* (England), 12 December 1986, 12.

Changes in women's employment rights will impact British women who are job sharing because most of them work no more than twenty hours per week--which means they will fall below the hours required for full-employment (maternity) rights.

791. Prior, Elaine. "A Rare Breed." *Social Work Today* 22 (30 May 1991): 20.

A female social worker shares a position with a male social worker (who spends his time away from the office raising pedigreed sheep). The job-sharing team keeps a joint diary to aid communication. (See item No. 801 for a related article.)

792. "Project JOIN in Second Year." *DOA Today* (Wisconsin Department of Administration) (September 1977): 4.

Wisconsin's Department of Administration has two positions that are shared as Project JOIN (Job Options and Innovations) begins its second year.

793. *Project JOIN (Job Options and Innovations)*. Madison, WI: Department of Employment Relations, State Division of Human Resource Services, Federal Manpower Programs Section, 1979. 2 vols.

This title consists of two volumes--a final report and a manual for replication. Project JOIN was established to develop and test job sharing in professional and para-professional positions in the Wisconsin civil service system. The final report covers implementation strategies and legislation in addition to summaries of positions and the research findings of fifty-six shared jobs. Appendices include employment rights and benefits, employee and private sector surveys, resume writing, and a bibliography. The manual for replication includes the following chapters: analysis of statutes, personnel and budget systems, setting up the program, and implementation as well as a summary and conclusions. Included also is a listing of shared positions that were researched.

794. Purnick, Joyce. "Koch to Modify 9 to 5 Jobs to Suit Needs of Employees." *New York Times*, 9 October 1980, B1.

The mayor of New York City tells his municipal agencies to formulate plans that allow for alternatives (flextime, compressed schedules, part-time, and job sharing) to the nine-to-five workday.

795. *Questions & Answers about Job Sharing.* St. Paul, MN: Department of Employee Relations [1983]. 3p.

These three fact sheets list questions and answers on the State of Minnesota's job-sharing program. Included are statements on who can participate, what positions may be shared, in addition to union dues, probationary periods, benefits, and salaries.

796. Rancer, Michael D. "Job Sharing: Two for the Price of One." *Management Information Service Report* (International City Management Association) (October/November 1977): whole issue.

This four-page report was prepared by an International City Management Association team that visited city officials in Palo Alto and Menlo Park, California, to discuss their job-sharing arrangements. Specific examples are given in addition to the advantages and disadvantages. The review team's assessment of the job-sharing experience concludes the report. One of their conclusions was that job sharing "offers a flexible, cost-effective way of utilizing municipal resources to meet the demands of its citizens."

797. *Report on Two-Year Pilot Job Sharing Project.* St. Paul, MN: Department of Employee Relations, 1981. 16p.

This office memorandum from Minnesota's Department of Employee Relations reports on the legislature-approved two-year pilot job-sharing project. It details the program implementation, what positions have been allocated, and the plans for evaluation. Copies of questionnaires for full-time and job-sharing employees are included.

798. Robinson, Bryan. "Surrey County Council." *Public Finance and Accountancy* (16 October 1987): 12.

Job sharing is proposed to the Surrey County council by women accountants who are returning to work after maternity leaves. The council accepts the proposal and makes plans to review the arrangements at the end of three months and again after twelve months.

799.   Sapper, David Bruce. "An Evaluation of Job Sharing among Minnesota State Employees: Productivity, Job Satisfaction and a Model for Development." M.A. thesis, University of Minnesota, 1983. 132p.

This thesis is a study of nineteen shared positions in the Minnesota State government with its thirty-six job sharers and their seventeen supervisors. The research focused on productivity, job sharers' satisfaction, and reasons for participation. Included in the literature review is information on job sharing in several states--California, Hawaii, Michigan, Minnesota, Oregon, Utah, and Wisconsin. Chapter topics include the environmental history of Minnesota's job-sharing program, job-sharer job satisfaction, supervisory perceptions of program success, and productivity results, including the effect of job sharing on quantity of work, quality of work, workflow, and overall performance. Copies of the questionnaires comprise ten appendices. Bibliography.

800.   Sawyer, Kathy. "Half-Year Stint Gives His Job More Zest." *Washington Post*, 25 December 1977, A15.

A parole officer in Madison, Wisconsin, shares his job by working six months on duty and six months off. He enjoys the free time during the summer because it gives him the opportunity to travel with his school-teacher wife.

801.   "Share and Share Alike." *Working for Sheffield* (England) (October 1986): unnumbered.

A man who runs a sheep farm and a woman who wanted to pursue additional education share the position of social worker for the Sheffield City Council. (See item No. 791 for a related article.)

802.   "Sharers Win Major Victory." *Work Times* [4] (Spring 1986): 3.

Co-directors of Region IX in the Women's Bureau, U.S. Department of Labor, are reinstated by the U.S. 9th Circuit Court of Appeals after being fired from their job-sharing position.

803. Shribman, David. "A Lesson for Voters: Two for the Price of One Is No Bargain." *Wall Street Journal*, 21 February 1990, A1+A9.

This is a peripherally related story on job sharing in state politics. The Indiana House of Representatives has one hundred elected members--fifty Republicans and fifty Democrats. Consequently, there are two speakers of the House, two principal clerks, and two chairpersons for all committees. Shribman says this "gives a whole new meaning to the term job sharing." Legislators complain it takes more time to do their work, resulting in the least efficient way to run a government.

804. Sidwell, Graham. "Job Splitting Threatens to Put Women Out of Work, Says Equality Commission." *Birmingham* (England) *Post*, 5 January 1983, 10.

The Equal Opportunities Commission in Britain has encouraged job sharing as a way of improving the status and quality of part-time work. They contend, however, that the government's job-splitting scheme will not accomplish those goals and may just be a means of reducing unemployment figures.

805. Stark, Gail. "Job Sharing Gets the Work Done." *Bellingham* (WA) *Herald*, 8 October 1989, C1+C3.

In addition to women city attorneys sharing one position in Bellingham, Washington, job sharing is taking place in Whatcom County where the position of probation officer is shared by a man and a woman. He previously worked as a police officer for twenty-six years and wanted to phase into retirement; she wanted to start a family. He receives medical benefits while she gets vision and dental coverage.

806. *State of Oregon 1977-79 Job Share Experience*. Salem, OR: Budget and Management Division, 1979. 47p.

This report summarizes the job-sharing program undertaken in the State of Oregon. It includes charts and tables that analyze the costs and benefits of job sharing and contains copies of the employment application, requests for certification, and letters from state agencies regarding job sharing.

807. Steenge, Ann-Marie, and Nancy Perozzo. "Job Sharing: A Creative Option." *Canadian Home Economics Journal* 34 (Summer 1984): 128-129.

The authors offer pointers to others wishing to introduce job-sharing positions into their organizations. Steenge and Perozzo are employed by the Manitoba Department of Health and share a community home economist position. Bibliography.

808. Stevens, Val. "Job Sharing Solves a Timely Problem." *Evening Echo* (Basildon, England), 7 October 1987, unnumbered.

Two British Health Service employees (women) share a position by dividing the work load two-thirds to one-third. One woman needs her free time for family activities while the other uses her time off to pursue a college degree.

809. Tendler, Stewart. "Yard Considers Job Sharing for Women." *Times* (London), 24 September 1987, 3.

Scotland Yard encourages its former policewomen to return to work on a part-time basis.

810. Thomson, Claude. "Region Studies Union Plans for Job Sharing." *Glasgow* (Scotland) *Herald*, 19 June 1985, 9.

The Strathclyde Regional Council is reviewing a job-sharing proposal announced by the National and Local Government Officers Association. Reasons for the union's interest in, and support of, job sharing are given.

811. United States. Congress. House. Committee on Government Operations. Manpower and Housing Subcommittee. *The Women's Bureau: Is It Meeting the Needs of Women Workers?* Washington, DC: U.S. Government Printing Office, 1984. 304p. ERIC, ED 250 579.

Included in these hearings is the testimony of two women who shared the position of regional administrator of the Women's Bureau for three years and were discharged in November 1983. Their testimony incorporates an overview of the regional administrator's duties, examples of projects and activities undertaken, and a description of the job-sharing arrangement.

812. United States. Congress. Senate. Committee on Labor and Public Welfare. Subcommittee on Employment, Poverty, and Migratory Labor. *Changing Patterns of Work in America, 1976.* Washington, DC: U.S. Government Printing Office, 1976. 497p. ERIC, ED 127 259.

Presented in these hearings are documents entitled "Job Sharing in the Schools" and "Job Sharing: A Guide to Developing a Job-Sharing Project" by New Ways to Work in Palo Alto, California. Also included is a bibliography, a chronology, and several pages of testimony by staff members of New Ways to Work and other people involved with job-sharing arrangements.

813. Vukelich, Dan. "Wolf to Seek Federal Job Sharing." *Washington Times*, 18 May 1989, B2.

Virginia Representative Wolf plans to introduce a bill that will make the federal government competitive with private industry by allowing federal employees to participate in job-sharing programs. The Office of Personnel Management would act as the clearinghouse.

814. Webster, Mary Helen. "Job Sharing: An Alternative Work Schedule." M.P.A. thesis, University of Wisconsin-Oshkosh, 1986. 92p.

After reviewing job sharing in general, this researcher identifies several hypothetical job-sharing settings for the Dodge County (Wisconsin) Department of Social Services. She provides a profile of current employees, work patterns, and interests in alternative work schedules as well as advantages and disadvantages to employees and supervisors. Bibliography.

815. Willis, Judith. "Union Issues Stall Public Sector Plans." *Minneapolis (MN) Star*, 26 November 1980, C1+C3.

Willis details several examples of experimental job sharing in Minnesota's governmental offices. Union concerns have centered around benefits and the union's fear the state will cut back on full-time jobs in order to provide additional shared positions.

816. *Work Sharing and Job Sharing in Michigan State Government--A Report.* Lansing, MI: Michigan Department of Civil Service, Office of Policy & Public Affairs, 1982. 52p.

The purpose of this paper is to report on work sharing and job sharing for employees of the Michigan classified civil service. A task force was established to study part-time employment and a survey (copy included) was mailed to 500 permanent part-time employees. Conclusions and recommendations concerning both options are outlined. Bibliography.

Unpublished Documents

817. "Job Sharing." London: National Association of Probation Officers, 1982. 5p.
    These pages list the advantages and disadvantages of job sharing for all branches of the London-based National Association of Probation Officers.

818. "Job Sharing: A Discussion Document." Edinburgh: Educational Institute of Scotland, 1982. 5p.
    This is a draft discussion of job sharing as applied to the teaching profession in Scotland.

819. "Job Sharing at the City of Ottawa: An Empirical Study." Ottawa, Ontario: Department of Human Resources, 1985. [27p.]
    Prepared by Ottawa's Department of Human Resources, this report examines job sharing theoretically and evaluates the city's job-sharing program.

820. ["Job-Sharing Policy."] Fort Collins, CO: Colorado State University, 1991. [5p.]
    These pages are from the Colorado State University Libraries policy manual.

821. ["Job-Sharing Policy."] Wichita, KS: Wichita Public Schools, 1990. [6p.]
    The Wichita Public Schools policy on job sharing and a sample job-sharing agreement are detailed in these pages.

822. "Job Sharing: Will It Work for You?" Fresno, CA: California Park and Recreation Society, 1986. 12p.

Included in this conference packet it information from several sources.

823. "Report of the Study Committee on Job Sharing for Group I Members of the New Hampshire Retirement System." Concord, NH: The Committee, 1990. [4p.]

This report was issued to clarify concerns of job-sharing teachers receiving credit for service in the New Hampshire Retirement System.

824. Stewart, Cheryl A., Jeanne L. Kennedy, Christine M. Sierra, and Charles W. Gossett. "Job Sharing in Municipal Government: A Case Study in the City of Palo Alto." Stanford, CA: Action Research Liaison Office, Stanford University, 1975. 17p.

This study, which investigated job sharing in the California city of Palo Alto, was the result of a political science class project. It was later condensed and published as an article. (See item No. 768.)

Addendum

825.   "Employment Law Problems: Job Sharing 1–General Aspects."
        IDS Brief (London) (June 1987): 7-10.
        In order to qualify for statutory rights covered in
        employment protection legislation, job sharers have to establish
        the necessary continuity of service. This means that sharing
        often must be half-day and half-week schedules. Other
        schedules (such as week on/week off, three-day week/two-day
        week) may not be considered for continuity of service and will
        jeopardize the sharers' employment rights. This article examines
        some of the legal implications of job-sharing contracts.

826.   "Employment Law Problems: Job Sharing 2–Sex Discrimina-
        tion." *IDS Brief* (London) (July 1987): 9-12.
        This article (a companion to item No. 825 above) explains
        why employers who turn down requests from women who wish
        to job share may be sued for indirect sex discrimination.
        Whether these cases are won or lost often depends on the
        employers and whether they can justify their reasons for refusing
        the job-sharing request. Included are descriptions of several
        cases that have gone to court.

827.   *Fair Shares: Making Job Shares Work,* edited by Mike Rosen
        and Patricia Leighton. London: Hackney Job Share, 1991. 92p.
        The editors of this book say that "1991 marks the start of a
        new phase for job sharing in the United Kingdom." Job sharing
        is being accepted by employers, trade unions, and workers at
        varying levels of responsibilities. This book is divided into two
        parts: making job sharing work and job sharing–employment
        law. Included in the chapters are the following topics: changing
        attitudes, can you afford to job share? how to apply, dividing the
        job, recruitment policies, employment rights, the contract, unfair

187

dismissal, and enforcing legal rights. Also included are the names and addresses of several groups or organizations interested in supporting the concept of job sharing.

828. Purdie, Helen, and Gillian Pincus. "Two for the Price of One: Job Sharing in a School Library." *Journal of the School Library Association of Queensland*. 14 (1982): 4-5.

The principal at St. James's Christian Brothers School in Queensland supports the idea of two people sharing the duties of one librarian. The sharers found their biggest problem was communicating with the teachers about assignments. They did, however, accept work on each other's behalf. Students tended to regard both librarians as one and often discussed what had happened on Mrs. X's day with Mrs. Y, as though Mrs. Y had also been there.

829. Wolfe, Melanie. "Job Sharing: Creating a Dynamic Duo!" *Four Star* (Smithsonian Institution Women's Council Newsletter) 9 (Summer 1989): 1-3.

Wolfe lists ten reasons for companies to introduce flexible work schedules and eight components of a comprehensive job-sharing plan that includes, among other things, a breakdown of job responsibilities, specific communication tools to be used, and how peak times, emergencies, and personal leave periods will be handled. Jobs suitable for sharing include ones that are "relatively independent or project-oriented, creativity-oriented, deadline-oriented, highly stressful or specialized."

Index
Numbers refer to entries, not pages.

About the Author

Thyra K. Russell is the Personnel and Order Librarian at Southern Illinois University at Carbondale. She earned her MLS from Northern Illinois University and Ph.D. from Southern Illinois University at Carbondale. Dr. Russell has published an annotated bibliography on various forms of alternative staffing in libraries and has written and spoken on the topic of job sharing in libraries. Her 1987 dissertation, "Job Sharing in Illinois Libraries," is a comprehensive study of job sharing in six types of libraries: college/university, community college, law, medical, public, and special libraries.